WHAT PEOPLE ARE SAYING ABOUT *CAMPAIGN CONFESSIONS*

There is joy in winning, but participating is what matters most in politics, as Lasch, a true insider, reveals in this fascinating account of backroom strategy and drama.
— BRIAN MULRONEY, 18th prime minister of Canada

Laschinger, an old pro, wisely observes that the most important element of each organization is the candidate, him or herself.
— BILL DAVIS, 18th premier of Ontario

Only fighter pilots have more thrills than campaign managers. Or, more accelerated ups and downs. John Laschinger's participation in a host of Canadian campaigns — leadership runs, elections — provincial, federal, and municipal — has dropped him many times into the vortex of Canadian politics. He has been the coach, organizer, strategist and "fashion adviser" for some of the first names in the Canadian edition of the world's oldest blood-sport: politics.
— REX MURPHY, Canadian and Newfoundland media gadfly (his word) and icon (my word)

Laschinger has penned a unique and remarkable manual, memoir, and how-to guide for deciding whom to support and how to actually make it work.
— HUGH SEGAL, chief of staff to Prime Minister Brian Mulroney, former senator, and current master of Massey College

John is a master of the techniques and strategies of political campaigning and shares them all in this book…. This is a most valuable contribution to Canadian political discourse.
— PRESTON MANNING, former leader of Reform Party of Canada and founder of Manning Institute

The book is a master class in winning at electoral politics but it risks making its author obsolete. If I had Lasch's book when I ran for national leadership, I might not have needed Lasch!
— JOHN CROSBIE, provincial and federal Cabinet minister and "father of Canada-U.S. Free Trade"

Told from the vantage point of the ultimate insider with his unique half-century of political experience, this is a one-of-a-kind book and well worth the read.
— EDDIE GOLDENBERG, senior political adviser and chief of staff to Prime Minister Jean Chrétien

When policy wonks and politics convene, wonks listen. Read this book.
— TOM KIERANS, Canadian business leader and financial, governance, and public policy expert

An insightful analysis of the backrooms of political campaigns over 45 years by one of Canada's most experienced election managers.
— BARRY KAY, associate professor of political science at Wilfrid Laurier University

Politics requires teamwork. Behind every successful political couple stands a successful campaign manager, and Lasch is one of the best.
— JANE CROSBIE, John Crosbie's partner for 62 years

John Laschinger is the consummate campaign manager. Smart, focused, and never distracted by the crises of the day.... Aspiring politicos of all ages would do well to learn from this political master.
— JOE CRESSY, Toronto city councillor, Trinity-Spadina

John gives us a rare inside look into some of our highest profile elections. He truly is one of Canada's leading political minds and strategist!
— ANDREW HODGSON, former Ontario PC executive director and long-time political organizer

I can only say a big "thank you" for providing both the political junkies like me and the broader electorate with your experiences in politics.
— PETER HERRNDORF, CEO, National Arts Centre

There is no one on the Canadian political scene who knows more about the running of political campaigns ... it is a foolish candidate who ignores John's advice. This book will be the bible for future campaign managers.
— BRUCE CARSON, former aide and adviser to Prime Minister Stephen Harper

CAMPAIGN CONFESSIONS

Tales from the War Rooms of Politics

JOHN LASCHINGER

with Geoffrey Stevens

Foreword by Peter Mansbridge

DUNDURN
A J. PATRICK BOYER BOOK
TORONTO

Editor: Dominic Farrell
Copy editor: Cy Strom
Design: Jennifer Gallinger
Cover design: Sarah Beaudin
Cover image: ©iStock
Printer: Friesens

Library and Archives Canada Cataloguing in Publication

Laschinger, John, author
          Campaign confessions : tales from the war rooms of politics / John Laschinger ; with Geoffrey Stevens ; foreword by Peter Mansbridge.

Includes index.
Issued in print and electronic formats.
ISBN 978-1-4597-3809-6 (hardback).--ISBN 978-1-4597-3653-5 (paperback).--
ISBN 978-1-4597-3654-2 (pdf).--ISBN 978-1-4597-3655-9 (epub)

          1. Laschinger, John. 2. Political consultants--Canada--Biography. 3. Campaign management. 4. Political campaigns. 5. Canada--Politics and government. I. Stevens, Geoffrey, 1942-, author II. Mansbridge, Peter, writer of foreword III. Title.

JF2112.C3L37 2016   324.7092   C2016-903432-1
                                                          C2016-903433-X

1 2 3 4 5   20 19 18 17 16

Conseil des Arts du Canada   Canada Council for the Arts   Canada   ONTARIO ARTS COUNCIL CONSEIL DES ARTS DE L'ONTARIO an Ontario government agency un organisme du gouvernement de l'Ontario

We acknowledge the support of the **Canada Council for the Arts** and the **Ontario Arts Council** for our publishing program. We also acknowledge the financial support of the **Government of Canada** through the **Canada Book Fund** and **Livres Canada Books**, and the **Government of Ontario** through the **Ontario Book Publishing Tax Credit** and the **Ontario Media Development Corporation**.

VISIT US AT
Dundurn.com | @dundurnpress | Facebook.com/dundurnpress | Pinterest.com/dundurnpress

Dundurn
3 Church Street, Suite 500
Toronto, Ontario, Canada
M5E 1M2

To Lucas and Sam

Contents

Foreword

by Peter Mansbridge

I've known John Laschinger for almost forty years. He's been there, done that, and got the political buttons and T-shirts to prove it from campaigns both at home and abroad.

But here's what's best about him. He has known winning *and* losing, and he's not afraid to talk about both. And that's a gift for us because there are lessons in the many stories you'll read in the pages that follow. Lessons for future candidates, lessons for future political strategists, but most important, lessons for us, the voters. Why do candidates act as they do? Why do those pamphlets you find at the door frame the issues the way they do? At what stage does a challenger know with a degree of certainty that he or she is going to win — or lose? Why do television ads take the approach they do? How has social media changed the game? Many of us have theories about the answers to these and many other questions, but Laschinger knows the real answers because he was there when the decisions were made to fight a campaign a certain way. He knows the joy of seeing a strategy work and the pain of watching it all fall apart. And he's not shy about telling us about both.

There is a lot of useful and important Politics 101 here, dealing with how things have changed because of twenty-first-century technology, but also how many things that worked in the nineteenth century still work today. But if you're a political junkie like me, what may fascinate you most will be the anecdotes of the backroom intrigue that "Lasch" has witnessed in his years of being at the heart of the story. Whether in federal elections, leadership races, provincial or municipal campaigns, he's seen a lot — some is pretty, some not so much. Politics can be ugly at times, and heartbreaking, too — you'll find it all here.

Will you have more respect for the system after you read what's ahead? Just as on voting day — that decision is yours.

Have a good read.

Acknowledgements

On New Year's Day 1990, my wife, Carol, and I attended a party at the home of Geoff and Lin Stevens to celebrate the arrival of the new year and decade. Geoff and I had just signed a contract to co-author a book about the backrooms of politics, *Leaders and Lesser Mortals*.

June Callwood, the celebrated Canadian journalist, author, and social activist, was also present that day. When she learned of our impending literary adventure she went out of her way to share her experience as a writer with us.

She compared writing a book to a relationship between a man and a woman. She said, "At the beginning everything is new, exciting, and wonderful. Then some drudgery sets in — the lustre and sparkle of the relationship starts to diminish as you find yourself staring at a keyboard for six or eight hours each day, often starting at dawn. Soon the process becomes ordinary and routine, just like a marriage. Then new obstacles and challenges arise. You may wish you could divorce yourself from the whole process before you get to the final chapter."

When June learned that the book that Geoff and I were co-authoring was the first book we'd tried writing together, she expressed her hope that our friendship would survive the experience. Twenty-six years later I can report that our friendship, which began in Ottawa in the 1970s when I was national director of the Progressive Conservative Party and Geoff was the national political columnist for the *Globe and Mail*, continues as we come to the end of our second collaboration.

Early in Olivia Chow's 2014 Toronto mayoralty campaign, which I directed, Geoff and I had a conversation about doing a second book together on politics once the campaign was completed. In early 2015 we reviewed three or four options before deciding that the approach that would make the book of greatest interest to readers would be to write it as an account of my fifty political campaigns — a memoir of my four-plus decades in the backrooms of politics.

As the manuscript evolved we realized that there were many stories from the campaigns that would interest political junkies, campaign operatives, and political scientists and their students. Why did John Tory and the Ontario Progressive Conservative Party really lose the 2007 provincial election, which became known as the "faith-based school-funding election"? What was the critical element that both allowed Rob Ford to win the mayoralty of Toronto and four years later cost him that position? How did my client, the president of Kyrgyzstan, get forced from office during the "Tulip Revolution" in 2005, and how did he end up where he is today — living in Moscow under Vladimir Putin's supervision? And how did Justin Trudeau go from third place in the polls at the start of the 2015 federal election campaign to the prime minister's office on election night?

We discussed our approach to the book with our friend Anna Porter, former CEO of Key Porter Books, who had published our first book. Key Porter had ceased to exist in 2011, but Anna was excited about a second political book from us, and she provided excellent advice as we wrestled with both the content and the choice of a publisher. She also provided suggestions regarding the content of the book. In particular, she advised us to include material from the 2015 federal election even though I had not been involved in the campaign. She felt the Canadian people had become caught up in that election and there would be a thirst for an analysis of the campaign and the forces that had driven the final result.

In addition to Anna, there were a number of individuals who provided content suggestions and advice during this project and/or took the time to read draft chapters: David Miller, Frank Ryan, Bret Snider, Hugh Mackenzie, Fraser Laschinger, Patrick Gossage, Hugh Segal, Greg Lyle, Mike Hurst, Tom Kierans, Tony Clement, Jennifer Hollett, Peter Herrndorf, Bob Gallagher, Stephen Pustil, Bruce Carson, Joe Pantalone, Bill Cronau, Ches Crosbie,

Acknowledgements

Andrew Hodgson, Gord Muschett, Dan Tisch, Eddie Goldenberg, Alastair Campbell, Sam Wakim, Jennifer Macpherson, Allan Gregg, Ahmad Ktaech, Kamil Baialinov, Donna Dasko, Jamey Heath, and Naheed Nenshi.

While others provided advice and views, I accept the responsibility for any errors or omissions. I did not have the advantage of a personal diary to work from, and, while I pride myself on having an excellent memory I may have missed something along the way or mis-recalled a detail of an event or conversation. I did have direct access to much of the research that I have referred to in various chapters and, of course, there is the Internet, an excellent source for dates and details.

While the stories are all mine, the book would not have been written as it is today without Geoff Stevens's contribution: his challenging and insightful questions regarding format and content, and his superb word-smithing. He is truly one of the best writers in Canada.

As chief correspondent for the CBC and anchor of *The National*, CBC television's nightly newscast for almost thirty years and as someone who knows the importance of the political process in a democracy, I feel especially privileged in having Peter Mansbridge write a foreword for my book.

I wish to thank Patrick Boyer for introducing our book to Dundurn. I wish to thank, too, the team at Dundurn for their role in producing this book. First and foremost, I want to thank my editor Dominic Farrell for his invaluable assistance during the development of the book. He found many ways to help improve the book and worked with me always in a prompt, responsive, calm, and sensitive manner. Carrie Gleason, the editorial director, oversaw the creation of the book, Kathryn Lane supervised the production of the book, and Cy Strom, the copy editor, helped with the fine-tuning of the manuscript. I also want to thank Michelle Melski, our publicist at Dundurn, for her work, which is ongoing, in helping me promote the book. To all, Geoff and I are most grateful.

My personal thanks go out to my family for all their support over the years. Carol has been endlessly patient and long-suffering. It wasn't a whole lot of fun being married to a political campaign manager who was often on the road on weekends and for extended periods during election campaigns. Thanks to my son Brett and his wife Neisha for giving Carol and me two wonderful grandchildren, Lucas and Sam. Perhaps the stories in this book will encourage them to follow their father, grandfather, and great-great-grandfather into politics and public service.

I want to thank our daughter Jan for being my biggest fan. She shows up to help at campaign offices and enthusiastically wears buttons or T-shirts to support my candidates.

Finally, I want to say a few things about my late parents. Elsa and Gordon Laschinger were great parents who lived for their children. While raising a middle-income family in Montreal, they somehow found the means to send all four of their children to private schools and university. They spent their money mainly on education, rather than travel, restaurants, or entertainment.

Politics was not a big topic of conversation in our home, and I don't remember Dad talking much about his father, possibly because he was just four years old when his father died. Only later did I learn of his father Edmund's important roles in politics and public service. I did know that he was considered a brilliant bureaucrat in Ottawa and later became a leading financier in Toronto. (The 1912 edition of the book *The Canadian Men and Women of the Time* contained a quotation from the *Toronto Star* describing Edmund as "a man of exceptional ability.")

My Liberal DNA. Edmund Laschinger, my grandfather, was an assistant to Ontario's Liberal premier Oliver Mowat in the 1890s and an adviser to Prime Minister Wilfrid Laurier on post office issues. When Edmund left government in 1911, the *Toronto Star* described him as "a man of exceptional ability." Edmund's close friend Mackenzie King became prime minister in 1921.

Acknowledgements

At some point I came to realize that Dad was a federal Liberal, as Edmund had been a friend of Mackenzie King when they were both federal civil servants in the years leading up to the First World War; as a result his mother had been a life-long Liberal, too. But my parents' support for their children knew no bounds — as Dad and Mother became staunch supporters of the Progressive Conservative Party and Michael Meighen, their candidate in Westmount, after I surprised them by being appointed PC national director in 1973.

Perhaps they could have anticipated my move to the PC Party if they had considered the other half of my political pedigree. Apart from my Liberal connections in the Laschinger family, there is also a Conservative connection with Sir John A. Macdonald who appointed the Hon. Sam Merner, my great-great-great uncle, to the Canadian Senate in 1887. Sam was the first Swiss-Canadian appointed to the Senate.

My Conservative DNA. Sam Merner, my great-great-great uncle, was a Member of Parliament from 1878 to 1882 and was appointed to Senate by Sir John A. Macdonald in 1887.

These days, few people view politics and politicians in a favourable light. However, after a lifetime of campaigns I still see politics as a noble calling for those in both the front and back rooms. Politics offers its practitioners unique opportunities to make real and positive differences in the lives of all of our citizens.

Introduction

Call Me Lasch.

My name is John Laschinger, but most people call me "Lasch."

I suppose you could say I am a political gunslinger. I run political campaigns and provide strategic advice to candidates or parties. To my knowledge, I am Canada's only full-time professional campaign manager. I have been at it for more than forty-five years, in which time I have been the manager, director, senior strategist, or adviser for fifty different campaigns, working at the federal, provincial, and municipal levels in Canada as well as overseas. My work has taken me to political wars from Victoria, British Columbia, to St. John's, Newfoundland, to Ottawa, to London, England, and to Bishkek, the capital of the former Soviet satellite of Kyrgyzstan.

Along the way I have had the privilege to work with politicians of every political stripe. Every campaign taught me something I, and frequently many others, did not know. I have tried to pass along these lessons and revelations to readers of this book. There are a few confessions, too.

Over the years and after working on so many political campaigns I've come to realize that two of the most important lessons — both applicable to the recent 2015 Canadian federal election — are the need to understand the desire for change and the need to manage the expectations for your candidate. While I was not directly involved in the 2015 federal election, I watched its developments closely. I'd like to say a few words about it here.

There is always an element in the electorate that believes the solution to all political problems is to throw the bums out, to get rid of the people in office and replace them with someone (or anyone) else. This is natural. It is normal. It is inevitable. And as long as this desire for change stays around the 50 percent level, it does not worry campaign managers for incumbents. But there is a magic number: that number is 60 percent. When pollsters start reporting that 60 percent of respondents believe it is time for change, campaign planners and managers know the handwriting is probably on the wall. When the number passes 60 and stays there, they know it is time to call in the movers and the document shredders.

Stephen Harper and the Conservatives knew they were in trouble long before they embarked on the 2015 campaign. After nearly a decade in power, they had alienated many voters and bored others. If ever there was time for a change, this was it. In the summer of 2015 most polls were reporting a "change number" in the range of 70 percent.

As for managing expectations, campaign organizers always prefer to deal with low expectations (because they have nowhere to go but up) rather than high expectations (nowhere to go but down).

The repeated advertising attacks on Justin Trudeau — "Just Not Ready" — by the Conservatives prior to the election call were effective to the extent that they helped drive down the public's expectations for the son of the former prime minister by the start of the campaign. With his party in third place and the leader deemed to be not ready for prime time, very little was expected of him.

I will be presenting a more detailed analysis of the reasons for Justin Trudeau's victory on October 19, 2015, in the first two chapters of this book.

The 2015 campaign was far in the future, however, when I made my first venture into politics. It was August 1971, and I was working for IBM in Toronto when I was introduced to the new premier of Ontario, Bill Davis. One week later I was a newly minted volunteer member of Ontario's Big Blue Machine. One month after that, I was a member of the

Left: *Meeting him changed my life.* A sketch of Ontario premier William Davis. The sketch was given to me by Davis as a thank-you for volunteer advance work in 1971 Ontario election. It is signed, "Best wishes, John – Bill Davis."

Below: *Those who party together stay together.* After the 1971 Ontario election, our "Dirty Dozen" advance group held semi-monthly lunches in preparation for our next assignment – with Robert Stanfield in the 1972 federal campaign. Here we are in the empty ballroom of Toronto's "King Eddy" Hotel.

"Dirty Dozen," as we called the team of advance men who prepared the way for Davis as he campaigned across Ontario. That provincial election campaign returned a majority Progressive Conservative government on October 21, 1971. Celebrating in Davis's house on Main Street in Brampton that night was a heady experience for a young salesman from IBM. It changed the course of my life.

The following year, 1972, I was again a volunteer, this time with the federal PC Party as an advance man for its leader, Robert Stanfield, in the campaign that came within two seats of defeating Pierre Trudeau and the Liberal government. Stanfield must have liked me because he asked me to become national director of the Progressive Conservative Party in Ottawa.

Within a few years I was running my first big solo campaign, helping Brian Peckford in his run for the provincial Progressive Conservative leadership in Newfoundland in 1979. When Peckford won the leadership (on St. Patrick's Day), he became the premier.

Winning with the help of a pen. Newfoundland's Brian Peckford was very difficult to photograph, so I commissioned a sketch of him to be used on pamphlets and buttons in the 1979 PC leadership campaign and in the subsequent provincial election.

These days I do not work for any particular party or march to any particular political drummer. Most of my clients are the candidates themselves. Some are Tories, others Liberals or New Democrats or independents, while some have been former communists who are trying to find their bearings in the strange world of democratic politics. If I like a candidate and respect his or her values, I will work for that person even if I do not think he or she can win. Some people argue that winning is everything in politics. I do not necessarily agree. To me, winning is the olive in the martini, the cherry on the sundae, a treat, a bonus for successful participation — and in a democracy, participation is everything. I respect people who care enough to try, even if they do not win. I will always work for good people.

This might be confusing to some. I recall Corey Mintz, writer for the *Toronto Star*, writing, "Laschinger is, depending on whom you talk to or which way the wind blows, the James Carville or Karl Rove of Toronto. He calls both lefty mayor David Miller and former conservative Premier Mike Harris by their first names."

My most recent campaign was for Olivia Chow in Toronto in 2014. Olivia is a New Democrat. She was the NDP Member of Parliament for Trinity-Spadina, a downtown constituency in Toronto, and the widow of the late leader of the NDP, Jack Layton, who became leader of the Opposition in the 2011 federal election. Olivia had been a member of Toronto City Council before she entered federal politics, and following the death of her husband she decided to return to municipal politics and run for mayor of Toronto. She asked if I would help as her campaign manager.

There was some irony in this. Back in 1991 when Jack Layton was a long-haired member of the radical left wing of Toronto City Council, he ran for mayor. The Conservatives and Liberals in the city were aghast at the prospect of a socialist mayor. He was defeated by my client, June Rowlands, a Liberal. Now, twenty-three years later, his widow was asking me to help to win the post her husband had failed to capture.

I wish I could report I was as successful at electing Olivia as I had been at defeating Jack, but it was not to be. When she entered the race, she became the instant front-runner. She was a fine, principled, and experienced candidate. She understood the diversity and complexity of Toronto. She had the people skills to be an exceptional mayor. The moment she declared her candidacy she became the odds-on favourite to win. But her campaign faded, for reasons I will discuss in more detail later. Just let me say here that she was a victim of some of the most appalling racist, sexist, and vulgar abuse I have had the misfortune to witness in my life in politics. It disgusted me. Much of it originated with the supporters of the Ford brothers — Rob Ford, the bombastic, drug-abusing outgoing mayor for the previous four years, and Doug Ford, his older brother who wanted to succeed him in the mayor's chair. A regular stream of hate mail arrived at Chow headquarters, including in the early weeks an envelope containing human feces. It was like that throughout the campaign. Two days before the election, a man on the street in downtown Toronto actually yelled at her, "Get the fuck out of here. This is Ford Nation, bitch."

Like her other supporters, I had hoped that the better instincts of Toronto citizens — decency, fairness, and respect for diversity — would shine through on election day. If they did, they did not shine brightly enough to help Olivia. She finished third, trailing both John Tory, the eventual winner, and Doug Ford.

Not all of my campaigns were as unsettling as that one. I was fortunate to be able to work with some of the leading politicians of the era — Robert Stanfield, John Crosbie, Peter MacKay, Brian Mulroney, and Joe Clark in Ottawa. Premiers Bill Davis and Mike Harris in Ontario, Brian Peckford in Newfoundland and Labrador, and David Miller in Toronto.

I will discuss my experiences with many of them in the chapters to come. These chapters highlight the important lessons I have learned on my political journey. Please put your political science textbooks away — you will not find this practical stuff in those learned texts. But as the book unfolds we will consider some of the important factors in political campaigns that help drive success or failure.

THE BOOK IN OUTLINE

I begin the book with the importance of recognizing the central role that the desire for change can play in an election. The need to manage expectations (and the benefit of being able to exceed expectations) follows. The campaign managers for both incumbents and challengers need to understand and react to that desire for change, and to manage (and, with luck, exceed) public expectations — and be able to anticipate what will happen when they do, or do not, exceed those expectations.

The next group of chapters describes the lessons I have learned about specific areas of campaigns. I will present the lessons in roughly the same order as a candidate or campaign manager would have to address them in developing a campaign.

The first two of these chapters focus on the candidate. I begin by addressing the importance of the homework that all candidates, regardless of gender, should complete before setting out on the rocky road to an election. What steps does a prospective candidate need to take to prepare for a campaign? It is not as simple as you may think. The would-be politician must look in the mirror. Is this person really ready to put his or her name on the ballot? To make the adjustments and sacrifices that the next weeks and months will require? Candidates need to be prepared before they commit to an election campaign, and there are benefits to be realized by investing time and effort in that preparation or homework.

The chapter that follows looks at the special obstacles that lie in wait for female candidates. Although male and female candidates face similar challenges, women must also overcome certain unique obstacles as they prepare for a campaign. The chapter on the particular issues that women in politics must deal with will examine those differences and suggest some homework that will help them.

Of course candidates cannot win elections without help, and the creation of a team or organization is an early priority. The next chapter focuses on the team behind the candidate.

As we move through the book, the focus shifts to the need for research and polling, and the requirement to use that research to define the values, vision, and policies required for political success.

Following that, the central role of communications is examined. To be successful, campaign managers must address certain specific communications issues — both internal issues necessary for effective dialogue with party workers, and external ones crucial for delivering the candidate's and/or party's message to the voting public. These include the importance of a campaign "war room" in this era of 24/7 communications; the role and increasing significance of social media — and its limitations as a campaign tool; and how and when to use negative advertising to advance the candidate's cause – and to know when it will hurt more than help.

From there, we will examine the power and influence of money in political campaigns.

Having a well-prepared candidate in place and observing the lessons in these chapters will improve the chances for success, but cannot guarantee it. There is one more crucial lesson to discuss. It is discipline. Lack of discipline on a campaign team is a prescription for disaster. In politics, as in others of life's pursuits, hanging together is infinitely preferable to hanging separately.

The next chapter of the book will take us briefly out of North America to describe what happened when I took the lessons from my Canadian experiences and marketed that expertise abroad. During the period 1995–2005 I helped the President of Kyrgyzstan and members of his family conduct two presidential campaigns, one parliamentary campaign, and one referendum. This chapter will describe my role in the political life of this former Soviet satellite.

Finally, I wrap up with a summary of the lessons from the earlier chapters and a listing of the three main observations I can make about politics after spending over forty years working in the trenches. I have a list of recommendations for would-be candidates and a few notes on some of the big political events I've had the privilege of being able to participate in.

I invite you to join me on a rollicking ride through the adventures — and long knives — of political campaigning. Together, we will discover how politics has, and has not, changed over the years. All of this through the eyes of Canada's veteran campaign manager who has seen it all.

Chapter 1

The Desire for Change

Become a student of change. It is the only thing that will remain constant.

— ANTHONY J. D'ANGELO,
American writer and educator

The desire for change is the strongest and most unpredictable emotion in election campaigns. Stephen Harper could attest to that! In 2015, despite the fact that approximately 70 percent of eligible Canadian voters had told pollsters they wanted change in Ottawa, the Conservatives tried hard to resist the tide.

On Sunday, August 2, 2015, Harper went to the governor general to dissolve Parliament early for the election to be held on October 19. He had two compelling reasons for doing this. First, he hoped the extra-long seventy-eight day campaign, with its correspondingly larger election expense limit, would give the Conservatives, who supposedly had deeper pockets than their rivals, the opportunity to flood the airwaves with negative advertising to exploit the public's doubts about the ability of the New Democrats and Liberals to govern the country. They hoped to move the change number down at least enough to survive with a minority government.

Second, Harper hoped to avoid the same fate that the Ontario Progressive Conservatives had experienced in 2014 when the public-sector unions had spent millions to defeat them and their leader, Tim Hudak, during the election period. The election laws in Ontario allow any third party to spend unlimited amounts during a campaign to attack or support a political party. While the federal election laws limit the amount that third parties can spend during the official campaign period to $150,000 in total, including a limit of $3,000 per electoral district, Harper was concerned about the unlimited amount of pre-campaign money that they would spend attacking him and his party over the summer if an election had not been called.

So, the election was called. The logical choice for disaffected voters would have been the Official Opposition party, the New Democrats. But voters are not so predictable. Instead, after weighing the alternatives during the long, eleven-week campaign, the people opted for the third party, the Liberal Party, led by the relatively inexperienced Justin Trudeau. The demand for change was so great that on October 19, 2015, they made Trudeau prime minister with a majority government.

The 2015 election was not atypical. The fundamental question facing voters in most elections is whether they want to replace their elected representative, or representatives. Candidates need to understand this. Incumbents and challengers alike need to appreciate the strength or level of the desire for change, understand the reasons for it, and try to come to terms with the type of change that will satisfy voters without exceeding their risk tolerance.

It is standard practice for a campaign manager at the start of a campaign, if not earlier, to schedule a retreat that involves a number of diverse individuals who are either involved directly with the campaign or are close personal friends and supporters of the candidate. The objective of the retreat is to develop a strategic plan for the campaign and to create the ballot box question.

Those who are directly involved with the campaign generally bring political experience to the table, while close friends serve to keep the outcomes of the discussion somewhat rooted in the reality of the candidate's beliefs, values, and track record. It is normal for a candidate to attend the opening portion of such a meeting. He or she should then leave to allow for a full and frank discussion of the subjects at hand.

The agenda for a strategic planning session might look something like the following:

- Introductory remarks by candidate and session facilitator
- Review of available research (public opinion and other). Time-for-a-change analysis is always required
- Discussion of the strengths and weaknesses of each of the candidates and parties
- Discussion of current political environment
- Creation of effective messaging:

  ○ Us on Us — What do we want to say about ourselves?
  ○ Us on Them — What do we want to say about our opponents?
  ○ Them on Them — What will they want to say about themselves?
  ○ Them on Us — What will they want to say about us?
  ○ Initial discussions about the ballot box question

The ballot box question is the question that a campaign manager wants to have foremost in the minds of the voters as they enter the polling stations on election day.

Naturally, all campaign managers try to define questions that will benefit their own candidates.

The desired ballot box question for a challenger usually focuses on the voters' desire for change. The desired ballot box question for an incumbent normally highlights the strengths or positive vision of that candidate or party and/or a message designed to blunt the forces of change by raising the risk level associated with change.

Once the ballot box question has been decided on, the campaign needs to settle on an overall campaign slogan for use on all campaign materials and in construction of the campaign platform. It is not an easy task to fashion a slogan that conveys in a few words the reason why the candidate should be elected. Life is always more complicated than that. In a number of recent campaigns, I can recall when the slogan for the campaign was not finally decided until the second or third phase of the election.

There are many examples of desire-for-change slogans that have been successful in various democracies. Some of my favourites are:

1911   **No Truck or Trade with the Yankees:** Robert Borden and the Conservative Party, used to defeat Wilfrid Laurier and the Liberals who were promoting freer trade with the United States

1946   **Had Enough?:** Republican Party, used to win the congressional elections

1972   **It's Time:** Australian Labor Party, used to win the Australian national election

1978   **Labour Isn't Working:** British Conservative Party, used to win the U.K. national election

1979   **It's Time for a Change. Let's Give the Future a Chance:** Joe Clark and the federal Progressive Conservative Party, used to win the national election

1980   **Make America Great Again:** Republican Ronald Reagan, used to win the presidential campaign (this theme was adopted by Donald Trump in the 2016 Republican presidential primary)

1997   **Britain Deserves Better:** Tony Blair and the Labour Party, used to win the U.K. national election

1999   **200 Days of Change:** Bernard Lord and the PC Party of New Brunswick, used to win the provincial election

2008   **Yes We Can:** Democrat Barack Obama, used to win the presidential campaign; Obama also used **Change We Can Believe In** during that election

2010   **Vote for Change:** David Cameron and the British Conservative Party, used to win the national election

In reviewing successful slogans that advocate change, it appears obvious that a successful message usually needs to be short (usually three words or less) and focused (one message not two). The message also needs to be grounded in research findings.

There are two memorable Canadian political slogans that were used by political leaders to survive strong forces of change in the last eighty years. Mackenzie King and the Liberals were successful at being elected in 1935 in the midst of the Great Depression with the slogan "King or Chaos."

Pierre Trudeau was less successful in 1972 when he and his Liberal Party used the slogan "The Land Is Strong." The slogan was seen as arrogant and was widely derided. The Liberals won re-election but were reduced to a minority government.

There is always a risk associated with trying to put too much into a slogan. Given a choice of multiple messages, voters might focus on the least important message. An example occurred in the 2008 Democratic presidential primary in the United States. After eight years of Republican President George W. Bush, the voters wanted change. Obviously, the Democrats especially wanted change.

Hillary Clinton campaigned on a message of experience and change, attempting to take a swipe at the less experienced Barack Obama. She started by promoting her thirty-five years of public policy experience. But Democrats found this confusing because experience is counter to change. She then used two change messages: "Change We Can Believe In" and "Change We Need." Each of these was a diluted change message as compared to the simple change message that Obama used.

Obama built his campaign around a single focused message — the need for change. In the early part of the primary he used over twenty slogans, each involving change ("Vote for Change," "Change versus More of the Same," "Our Time for Change," etc.). His primary slogan later became "Yes We Can." Obama became the agent of change the Democrats wanted; he became the Democrat nominee and later the forty-fourth President of the United States.

More often than not, I have been involved with campaigns that advocate change. As a political professional, the odds are much greater that I will receive a telephone call for help from a candidate who is 40 percent behind than from one who is 40 percent ahead!

DEFINING THE DESIRE FOR CHANGE

The need to understand the voters' desire for change strongly suggests the need for both quantitative and qualitative research in the creation of a strategic plan, ballot box question, and campaign slogan.

Quantitative research will determine the level of change required, while qualitative research will provide insights into the details of change desired and the risks associated with change. The standard question asked of voters in a quantitative survey is:

> Some people say that (the incumbent leader/party) has done a good job in the past four years and deserve(s) to be re-elected. Others say that they have done a poor job and that it is time for a new leader/party to take over government. Which of these two positions is closer to your own?

The rule of thumb in interpreting the results of this question is that a leader or party will lose government when more than 60 percent of voters say they want change. (This is in contests where there are three main parties.)

The research results will dictate the strategies for both incumbents and challengers, as each should either be trying to lower or to raise the level of desired change.

As will be described in Chapter 12 on the need for discipline, the Ontario Liberals won the 2007 provincial election as a result, in part, of the relatively low level of change desired by the voters. On the eve of election day, just 50 percent said they wanted change, and 40 percent said the Liberals should be re-elected. On October 10, the Liberals won a majority government with 41 percent of the popular vote. The 50 percent that wanted change split their votes among the opposition parties. (This and many other examples are used by proponents of proportional representation as they seek to eliminate the first-past-the-post ballot system.)

I had a personal experience in June 1999 when I telephoned Bernard Lord, leader of the New Brunswick PC Party, on the weekend before the June 7 provincial election. I had the results of our previous night's polling, and for the first time our nightly tracking showed that the time-for-a-change level had reached 60 percent. At the beginning of the campaign, I had explained the need to reach that level in order to win. I started my conversation that weekend by addressing Lord as "Mr. Premier." Two days later, Bernard Lord and his Progressive Conservatives won a majority government.

A number of supplementary questions can be asked that explore the desire for change in both quantitative and qualitative research. These questions include:

When the desire for a change reaches the magic 60 percent. This 1999 photo shows me with premier-elect Bernard Lord in his office in the New Brunswick legislature in Fredericton. Lord is holding the nightly tracking done by myself and Northstar Research Partners during the campaign.

- Would you say that (Canada/your province/your city) is better off, worse off, or has there been no change in the years since the last election?
- Would you say that your community is better off, worse off, or has there been no change in the years since the last election?
- Would you say that you personally are better off, worse off, or has there been no change in the years since the last election?
- Do you think your children will be better off than you in the future?
- Do you think there needs to be a little change, a lot of change, or no change at all in the current government?
- In your opinion, how risky will it be to change government? Very risky? Somewhat risky? Or not risky?
- Would you say that overall the government of (Canada/your province/your city) is headed in the right or wrong direction?

The responses to these questions provide insights that flesh out the reasons for or against change and help describe the change that is required. Qualitative research can then be used to explore the following:

- What changes do you think need to be made? Why?
- If you were the head of government, what changes would you make on your first day in office? Why?
- Would you be very concerned, somewhat concerned, or not concerned at all if the current government were to be changed? Why?
- What would be your reaction to the following changes? Would you have a favourable, neutral, or unfavourable reaction to these potential changes? Why? (Respondents are provided with lists of possible changes.)

The results of the research are then matched with the candidate's values and track record to form the messaging, platform, and ballot box question for the campaign as it develops.

In the case where a challenger has more than 60 percent of the electorate wanting change, the campaign objective is to define what change might look like: "This is what you will get if you vote for me." The following are examples that have worked for these challengers:

- In Ontario in 1995, Mike Harris defined change with his platform "the Common Sense Revolution," which contained personal tax cuts and reduced welfare benefits.
- In the United Kingdom in 1997, Tony Blair defined change as the devolution of powers to the people of Wales and Scotland and an increase in the minimum wage.
- In New Brunswick in 1999, Bernard Lord defined change as the end to collecting tolls on the province's Trans-Canada Highway and by promising two hundred days of change during which he would deliver on twenty specific promises. (The initial slogan proposal was for one hundred days, but at the last minute Lord wisely decided that it was going to take longer to deliver on his promises.) After two hundred days in office he was able to proudly announce that nineteen of the twenty promises had been completed, and substantial work had been done on the twentieth.
- In Toronto in 2003, David Miller defined change as stopping the building of a bridge to the Island Airport and the ending of corruption at city hall.
- In Toronto in 2010, Rob Ford defined change as stopping the "gravy train" at city hall.
- In Alberta in 2015, Rachel Notley defined change as reversing the spending cuts that the previous

government had made to education and health care, combined with a balanced budget she promised by 2017.

Each of these definitions of change succeeded because each was simply defined and communicated after the campaign had paid close attention to the research findings.

The objective for a challenger when less than 60 percent of the electorate says it wants change is to drive up the change numbers. Here are two vivid examples where that was done during an election campaign.

In the federal election of 1993, Liberal leader Jean Chrétien won a resounding victory over Kim Campbell and the Tories. The Liberals had entered the election period statistically tied with the Conservatives, but the early release of campaign promises (through the Liberal Red Book, which included a promise to eliminate the unpopular Goods and Services Tax — Chrétien declared he would "axe the tax"), combined with a very poorly run Conservative campaign, helped propel Chrétien into the prime minister's office.

In New Brunswick in 2006, Liberal leader Sean Graham used the public's upset with provincially regulated auto insurance rates to drive up the time-for-a-change numbers and oust incumbent premier Bernard Lord. Graham and the Liberals had entered that election with polls showing them trailing Lord's Conservatives.

However, there are also a number of incumbents who have successfully rebuffed the winds of change with simple actions and slogans.

In Ontario in 1971, Premier Bill Davis won a majority government by cancelling the extension of the Allen Expressway into downtown Toronto and by announcing that full funding would not be granted to the Catholic school system past the then currently funded Grade 9 level.

In 1974, Liberal prime minister Pierre Trudeau won a majority government by saying to Canadians "Zap! You're frozen!" in opposition to the wage and price control policy being proposed by the Progressive Conservatives. Lack of discipline in the Tory ranks also helped Trudeau considerably.

The Desire for Change

In Newfoundland in 1982, Premier Brian Peckford won re-election with a slogan — "For Strong Leadership" — which backed up his record of standing up to the federal government in the fight for control of the province's offshore oil and gas resources.

In 1988 Prime Minister Brian Mulroney won a second majority government by supporting free trade with the United States.

In Kyrgyzstan in 2000, as we will see in Chapter 13, President Askar Akayev won a resounding victory by making Russian an official language of the country and cutting taxes for small businesses. (He was also helped by the criminal charges that the Kyrgyz KGB laid against his main opponent.)

In Ontario in 2007, Liberal Premier Dalton McGuinty won a majority government using the slogan "Change That Is Working" to describe the improvements he had made in the province, and (as we shall see in Chapter 12) he was helped significantly by the lack of discipline shown by some members of the Tory campaign.

In my experience, voters normally decide prior to an election that they want change; they either determine what change they want well ahead of the election, or they use the campaign period to make that decision. I have participated in, or observed, examples of both.

Consider the election for mayor of Winnipeg in 1992. David Brown had asked for my assistance following my client June Rowlands's victory in the Toronto mayoralty race in 1991. David was a well-respected Winnipeg city councillor, and months before the election we conducted a quantitative survey of likely voters in Winnipeg. The results were astounding. Each of the city councillors who were intending to run, or were rumoured to be running, to replace long-time mayor Bill Norrie, was trailing well behind Susan Thompson. Susan was a businesswoman who ran a small retail store in downtown Winnipeg and had never previously been elected. The voters were deeply unhappy with the city council and wanted change. Brown entered the race despite the numbers, and finished a distant third behind the winner Thompson. The voters had decided what change looked like well before the election started.

The 2010 mayoralty contest in Toronto provided a similar lesson. David Miller had been mayor since 2003 and initially had been successful on a number of major files — cleaning up corruption, managing the finances of the city, and creating plans for an expansion of the public transit system called Transit City. Then in the summer of 2009 there was a thirty-nine-day garbage strike. By late summer, 80 percent of the voters, perhaps driven by the smell of garbage rotting in city parks, reported to an Ipsos Reid survey that they wanted a new mayor. In the aftermath, Miller announced in September 2009 that he would not be a candidate for mayor in 2010. (He told me later that he had decided not to run again in 2010 on the evening that he was re-elected in 2006. He had grown weary of the negativity at city hall.)

I accepted an invitation by Deputy Mayor Joe Pantalone to manage his mayoral campaign. Joe had been a councillor for thirty years and had been very loyal to Miller. I understood that Joe's campaign would be seen by many as a continuation of the Miller policies and ideas, and frankly that is why I decided to work for him. I thought then, as I do today, that Miller had been a great mayor for Toronto, the garbage strike aside. (Many Torontonians, obviously, had changed their minds about the man and had come to that same conclusion, as a poll in September 2010, two months before the election, suggested that he would have been re-elected if he had been a candidate.)

However, with Miller gone it seems that voters, after considering the list of candidates who were running to replace him, had decided early that they wanted real change. That strong desire for change in early 2010 made it very difficult for Joe to gain traction, and he remained mired in third place throughout the campaign. Voters in that election used the campaign period to decide what change in the mayor's office should look like.

They had a choice between Rob Ford, a right-of-centre, small-government, penny-pinching, ten-year city councillor, and George Smitherman, a Liberal, left-of-centre, openly gay politician, who had served as both the former deputy premier and the health minister of Ontario. Along with his high-profile past, Smitherman also had a checkered financial management record as a result of the eHealth spending fiasco during his time as minister. So, when he resigned these positions to run for mayor, he had to deal with the considerable amount of baggage that accompanied him.

With two weeks remaining in the election voters had not yet made up their minds. I conducted a quantitative survey and found that Ford and Smitherman were statistically tied, 38 percent to 35, respectively, while Pantalone was at 22 percent. I watched in some amazement over the next two weeks as 9 percent of the left-of-centre Pantalone's support went to the right-of-centre candidate Ford, and just 1 percent went to the left-of-centre Smitherman. Pantalone's support was squeezed during the last two weeks, and on election day he received just 12 percent of the vote. I came to understand that the right/left labels do not matter much to the average voter. They were just leaving one populist, lefty Pantalone, to vote for another populist, conservative Ford.

Ahmad Ktaech worked with me on Pantalone's campaign and produced the visual look and branding for the campaign as well as the campaign materials. He thinks that there may be a more fundamental shift in politics that is emerging. "Politics as entertainment is a reality. Rob Ford entertained. Anyone who doesn't play to that risks losing." In support of this shift he also points to the recent 2016 Republican primary contest.

Joe Pantalone later commented upon what had happened in 2010. "The elites — the media, money people, and those in power — did not understand what was happening in the outer burbs, North York and Scarborough, with the challenges that the working-class voters in those areas were facing. They were working harder and still falling behind. They heard stories about councillors getting free coffee and lunches, and were attracted to Ford's penny-pinching message." A great divide had been created in Toronto between the elites and those living in the outer burbs.

The voters in Toronto during the 2014 mayoral campaign followed a similar change timeline to that in 2010. They had decided well in advance of the election period that they wanted a new mayor, as the time-for-a-change number stood at 66 percent for the better part of eighteen months prior to the election. Voters then used the first part of the campaign period to determine what this change should look like. In the next chapter I describe the events of that campaign, leading to the election of John Tory as mayor. The voters decided that Tory would be their agent of change in early July, well ahead of the October election. (It is of some note that the change numbers did not move at all during the

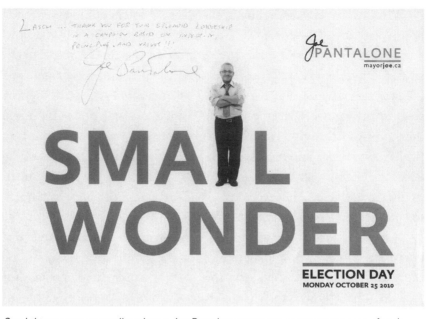

Good things come in small packages. Joe Pantalone campaign poster given to me after the 2010 mayoral race. The inscription reads, "Lasch: Thank you for your splendid leadership in a campaign based upon integrity, principles and values! Joe Pantalone."

campaign. Doug Ford, pinch-hitting for his ailing brother Rob, received 34 percent of the votes cast.)

Voters in the 2015 Alberta provincial election followed the 1992 Winnipeg mayoral change timeline. They decided well in advance of the election that they wanted Premier Jim Prentice and his PC government replaced, and they also decided before the election was called that they were prepared to elect Rachel Notley, leader of the NDP, as premier. While it appeared to take most pollsters in Alberta some time to figure out that the NDP were going to win, Notley recalled seeing the results of a poll from a well-respected pollster that had her party in the lead in the week before the election was called.

Afterwards I had the opportunity to talk with a pollster who had conducted surveys during that election. He told me that while Notley may have seen some positive NDP results early, he personally was surprised at the results of a poll that was conducted the day the election was called. It had the NDP winning. He was not sure of the accuracy of those results, so two riding surveys were quickly conducted. The NDP was tied for the lead in Medicine Hat (a riding the party had never won) and was winning in the riding of St. Albert by a huge margin. On May 5, Rachel Notley became premier-elect of Alberta.

A QUESTION OF TIMING

Little research has ever been conducted in Canada to determine when voters make their decision on whom to vote for. I had the opportunity to conduct that type of research in 2002, following two Ontario provincial by-elections. Keeping in mind that polls are just a snapshot at a point in time, the results are thought provoking and deserve consideration by campaign managers in their campaign budget-allocation decisions.

The results showed that there were three categories of voters in the two by-elections:

- Early deciders — 36 percent said they knew whom they would support prior to the election call
- Mid-campaign deciders — 39 percent said they made up their minds midway through the campaign
- Procrastinators — 25 percent said they made up their minds in the last few days of the campaign, with 9 percent not deciding until election day

These results should have a significant impact upon the timing of the allocation of campaign resources. They support the theory of a U-shaped campaign-spending curve, with sufficient resources being allocated both before the call of an election and in the closing days of a campaign. (There is little a campaign manager can do to reach the laggardly 9 percent other than scratch his or her head in frustration.)

As I have noted, a recent example of the impact of time-for-a-change occurred in the 2015 Canadian federal election. Prime Minister Stephen Harper had been in office since 2006, although he had had a majority government only since 2011. During the early part of 2015 polls revealed extreme dissatisfaction with the Harper government, and for much of that time the NDP under their new leader Tom Mulcair was in the lead. While there was no public reporting of time-for-a-change numbers during that time, it is reasonable to deduce what the level was from the level of support reported for the Harper Conservatives heading into the campaign. The first poll published after the call of the election on August 2 had the Conservatives at 28 percent. It is reasonable to assume the time-for-a-change number was then approximately 72 percent.

A number of polls in late July and early August placed support for Tom Mulcair and the NDP between 34 and 39 percent, and Justin Trudeau and the Liberals between 23 and 29 percent, with the Conservatives and Harper in the 28 to 33 percent range. It is very likely that the time-for-a-change number was between 67 and 72 percent as the campaign started.

The first published change number came in early September when Nanos Research reported that the number was at 69 percent. This was well above the 60 percent level that insiders deem necessary to defeat a government.

Harper as the incumbent chose a slogan to emphasize his strengths — "Proven Leadership for a Strong Economy."

He responded to the high change numbers by using scare tactics against the Liberals and the NDP. He said that Mulcair and Trudeau would be disasters as prime ministers, with higher taxes and large government deficits. He also picked a fight against Muslim women wearing the niqab when they took the oath of Canadian citizenship, a fight that he lost in Federal Court in early October.

He did little to provide new ideas in his platform. He did work at solidifying his current base of support by promising future balanced budgets, continuing his support for previously announced initiatives — income splitting, an increase in tax-free savings account (TFSA) contributions to $10,000 per year, continuing Canada's military role in the bombing of Islamic State enclaves in Iraq and Syria, and protecting Canadians from terrorists at home. In the second-to-last week of the election, the Conservatives announced they would set up a "snitch line" to the RCMP for Canadians to report their discovery of any "barbaric cultural practices." All of these measures appeared to solidify the Conservatives' support in the 31 to 34 percent range toward the end of the campaign. But Harper's basic message to all Canadians wanting change was: "Vote for me, and you will get more of the same and we will stay the course." The Conservatives also ran a series of negative ads against both the NDP and the Liberals, including the "Just Not Ready" ad that had worked so well for them in the pre-writ period to pull the Liberals down into third place.

The Conservative attack ads did not work. Most voters either ignored or discounted them as a desperation tactic. In the days immediately before the election, the change number was still at 71 percent.

It can be argued that the Harper Conservatives, because of the profound desire for change, had actually lost the election before it began, and that their negative campaign simply sealed their fate because it reminded voters of all the reasons why they wanted to get rid of Harper.

Mulcair and the NDP settled on a campaign slogan "Change That Is Ready," in a thinly veiled jab at the less experienced Liberal leader, Trudeau. Mulcair was attempting to use his thirteen years of experience in elected office in Quebec to his advantage. He also had gained a good reputation on the Ottawa scene for being an effective opposition leader in the House of Commons. (Comparison of the NDP slogan to the 2008 Hillary Clinton primary-contest messaging shows an eerie similarity.)

In order to make the NDP seem less scary to voters, Mulcair decided to embrace Harper's promise of balancing the federal books if elected. However, in addition, he promised large expenditures for increases in health-care transfers to the provinces, an increase in the federal minimum wage, a universal daycare program and a universal pharmacare plan. He proposed to balance the books with modest increases in corporate taxes.

He appeared to be trying to be all things to all people and looked to some as if he stood for nothing. Worse, he alienated his progressive base. But much worse for Mulcair, he provided an opening that allowed Justin Trudeau and the Liberals to become the party of change that the large majority of Canadians wanted.

The Liberal campaign slogan was "Real Change." Trudeau proposed to increase the amount spent on infrastructure projects by $10 billion per year for three years and to run modest deficits during that time before returning to balanced budgets by 2019. He proposed to cut income taxes for the middle class and to raise taxes on the top 1 percent of wage earners. He also placed a number of smaller, more cosmetic changes into his platform responding to concerns about election laws, openness and transparency in the federal government, and increased accountability.

The movement in the NDP polling numbers told the story of which party was being seen as best representing change.

For the first three-plus weeks of the eleven-week campaign, Mulcair and the NDP led most polls, with support in the 30 to 39 percent range. The Conservatives were second. The Liberals were third.

During the middle part of the campaign, the NDP lost their lead and settled back into a statistical tie with the Conservatives and the Liberals. Each party had approximately 30 percent support. The Liberals had picked up support from voters who were leaving the NDP.

The NDP vote then did a second drop, and by September 28 their support had fallen to 27 percent. They were clearly in third position.

Two factors appear to have accounted for the NDP slide. They were no longer seen as representing the change that Canadians wanted and, second, Mulcair took a principled stand supporting the right of Muslim women to wear a niqab during their Canadian citizenship ceremony. Stephen Harper, always on the lookout for a wedge issue, had opposed their right to do so. Even after losing a court decision, Harper continued the fight by announcing that the government would appeal. He then extended the fight with a promise that no government employee would be allowed to wear a niqab while serving the public. The principled stand by Mulcair hurt the NDP with its base in Quebec where public opinion was running strongly against the niqab. (Trudeau and the Liberals took essentially the same position, but the NDP suffered the damage.)

By October 13, NDP support nationally had dropped to 23 percent.

The New Democrats remained buried in third place and were no longer serious contenders for the gold medal. They had failed to offer the change expected by the vast majority of Canadians.

By October 13, the Liberals had assumed a commanding 6 to 7 percent lead over the Conservatives. Around the time they sat down for Thanksgiving dinner, Canadians made their choice of the party that best represented their hope for change.

An exceptionally heavy turnout at the advance polls over the Thanksgiving weekend sent a strong signal of the verdict to come, as 3.6 million voters cast early ballots — 71 percent more than in the 2011 election. High turnouts are almost always bad news for incumbents.

On the final weekend Harper concluded his campaign with a rally in Etobicoke that was attended by Rob and Doug Ford. A photo of the embattled prime minister with the Ford brothers went viral, delighting Harper's core supporters and appalling many other Canadians. Over the weekend, I heard normally mild-mannered Canadians express their disgust at Harper being seen in public with Rob Ford. I suspect that Harper was just being loyal to a fervent supporter. By that time he knew the game was over.

When Trudeau and the Liberals won a solid majority government on October 19, most election watchers were surprised, but not Nanos Research. The Nanos polling in the final three days of the election had shown the NDP vote continuing to drop, to 19 percent, while the Liberals continued their upward momentum.

The low level of expectations for Trudeau entering the campaign certainly helped the Liberals. Much of the "credit" for those low expectations goes, ironically, to the Conservative war room with its too-clever "Just Not Ready" ads.

The Liberals sealed their victory with their ability to convince voters that they alone represented the change the country was demanding. The extra-long campaign worked to their advantage. The youngest and most vigorous of the leaders, Trudeau seemed to be everywhere in those frenetic seventy-eight days — trekking up Grouse Mountain in Vancouver, sparring in a boxing ring, or canoeing on the Bow River in Calgary, when he was not debating the other leaders on television or exciting Liberal faithful at party rallies. Trudeau seemed to grow stronger with each appearance.

Not expecting much initially, voters were pleasantly surprised. The long campaign gave more Canadians a chance to see and hear Trudeau, and the more they saw and heard the better they liked him, and they came to decide for themselves that he might just be ready. He could not be dismissed as a shallow pretender to the prime ministry. He was the real goods promising real change.

Once voters make up their minds that they want change, they typically express it in a decisive way — with a massive swing away from the incumbent and to the party or candidate that best represents the kind of change they want. When voters want change, they also typically do not want incremental change: they want diametrical, wholesale change. They tend to gravitate to the party or candidate that offers the cleanest break from the status quo.

We saw an expression of this in the 2014 Toronto mayoral campaign, where voters swung between two extremes: replacing Rob Ford, a crack-smoking, drunken, unkempt mayor with his polar opposite John Tory, a buttoned-down, blue-blood "suit" from one of Toronto's prominent society families.

In the 2015 federal election, the Liberals did a much better job than the NDP in identifying and articulating the kind of change that voters wanted. They understood that what they wanted was not just a change in policy, but in attitude, tone, values, and style of governing. Voters had had enough of the Harper approach — arrogant, bitter, mean-spirited, divisive, relentlessly partisan, and obsessively secretive. Justin Trudeau's "Sunny Ways" struck the opposite chord of openness, fairness, and inclusiveness.

When voters want change, opposition leaders should not get caught halfway in the middle, as the NDP did in 2015. As the Welsh politician Aneurin Bevan said in 1953, "We know what happens to people who stay in the middle of the road. They get run down."

And when voters want change, the governing party should offer it. It is doomed if it promises more of the same, as Stephen Harper and the Conservatives discovered in 2015.

Not only is there a political cost for parties that fail to satisfy the voters' desire for change, there is also fallout for the leaders of those parties. Acknowledging his failure in ensuring the Conservatives maintained their grip on power, Stephen Harper stepped down as party leader on election night. Tom Mulcair stayed on as leader, however, trying to convince his party that its desire for future success would be best served by sticking with him. But like the country's voters who wanted a clean break with the past, the party's members decided that a new beginning was needed, and six months after the election Tom Mulcair was forced out as NDP leader in a leadership review vote.

The level of desire for change has a major impact on the outcomes of most elections. A second, closely related factor also drives political success. It is public expectations — specifically, how the performances of the parties and candidates stack up against the expectations of voters. Politicians who meet or exceed expectations win elections; those who fail to measure up are the losers in election after election. The next chapter examines the impact of expectations on several recent elections.

Chapter 2

Managing Expectations

Life is largely a matter of expectations.
— HORACE, Roman lyric poet

In every political campaign voters, consciously or unconsciously, measure performance against expectations when they cast their ballots.

Winning campaigns are campaigns that meet or exceed the expectations of pollsters, pundits, and the voting public. Losing campaigns are campaigns that fall short of expectations.

It is also like that in life outside of politics. Performance in comparison to expectations plays a crucial role in the success or failure of individuals, commercial products and organizations, and prices of shares on stock exchanges, as well as in the rise or fall of political parties and candidates.

For a campaign manager, the management of expectations is an all-important task.

Expectation management is not just about avoiding errors that could lead to failure. It is also about creating opportunities to beat expectations and to achieve success.

Everyone connected with a political campaign, however tangentially, has expectations, and one of the trickiest tasks for any campaign manager is to keep the campaign in balance — to manage the expectations and to prevent them from running away with the campaign. It is the campaign manager's job to keep the organization on an even keel; to prevent candidates (and their workers and supporters) from becoming either dangerously overconfident or profoundly discouraged; to keep financial supporters reasonably content; and to try to make sure the media does not become either too excited or too skeptical about the candidate's prospects. It is especially critical not to make claims of exaggerated support that will come back to bite you later when the claims do not materialize. Short-term gains can often lead to long-term pain.

It does not take much to make expectations soar or plunge. A single opinion poll can change the mood. One debate can do it, or a television report, or the reaction of the audience — be it enthusiastic or hostile — at a crucial campaign meeting. Everyone looks to the campaign manager to strike and maintain that elusive balance between hope and reality.

Over the years, I have been involved with campaigns facing high expectations (front-runner campaigns, as we call them) and low expectations (challenger or long-shot campaigns). Each of these campaigns requires a different strategy. For a front-runner campaign, the questions are: How do you take advantage of your initial strength without looking as though you are taking the outcome for granted? And how can you dampen expectations so that by election day you can be in a position to exceed them?

For a challenger campaign, the question is quite different: How do you take advantage of low expectations?

The outcome of the 2015 federal election was greatly influenced, first, by the strong desire for a change from the Harper Conservatives, as described in Chapter 1; and second, by the low expectations that voters had of Justin Trudeau going into the campaign, combined with his performance during the writ period, which was widely seen to exceed those low expectations. (More about that toward the end of this chapter.)

I have seen several examples of how a campaign manager can try to take advantage of, or manage, low expectations heading into an election.

1990 ONTARIO PROVINCIAL ELECTION

On May 12, 1990, Mike Harris became the leader of the Ontario PC Party in a leadership contest that for the first time in its history allowed every party member to vote. I had managed Harris's leadership campaign and accepted his invitation to manage the Ontario PC Party's campaign in the next provincial election, expected in 1991.

But David Peterson started to have other ideas about the timing of the election. David Peterson was the Liberal premier at the time and was extremely popular. Poll results during the summer of 1990 put Peterson's Liberals at 48 percent, well ahead of the Ontario NDP at 32 percent and much further ahead of the Ontario PC Party at 18 percent. He calculated that his best opportunity for re-election might be in September of 1990. He was counting on the Conservatives and their new leader to be ill prepared for this quick call. He was right.

Hearing rumours of an early election, I invited Mike Murphy, a well-known Republican strategist, to visit Toronto in July and give us his independent assessment of our situation and some recommendations. Murphy was highly regarded and was especially well known for the television ad that the Republicans under George Bush Sr. had run against Democrat Michael Dukakis in the 1988 presidential campaign. The ad showed Willie Horton, a convicted murderer serving a life sentence, going out through a revolving prison door on weekend furlough in Massachusetts while Dukakis was governor of the state. Horton later committed a rape and assault while out of prison. Murphy went on to be a political consultant for a number of prominent Republicans including Arnold Schwarzenegger, Christine Whitman, John McCain, Mitt Romney, and Jeb Bush.

I arranged for him to meet with key members of our campaign team, and at the end of the day I met with him.

He started with his overall assessment. "You are in a great position!" he said.

Taken aback, I said, "How can that be? We are $5 million in debt. We have very few candidates. We have a leader who is not known by the electorate. We are 30 percent behind the Liberals. And we could be facing an election in a few weeks."

He said, "That's right. You have nothing to lose. You can be truly dangerous!"

After putting him back on the plane to Washington, I started to wonder how I could be truly dangerous.

Our research had shown that an early election call would be very unpopular with the voters. The public never says that elections are something they want and, when provided with the price tag of conducting this election, $30 million, they were that much more negative toward the early election.

The election laws of the time did not allow any advertising by political parties either in the first seven days of a campaign or in the last twenty-four hours. However, there were no limitations on advertising before an election was called. I knew that with our limited funds we would be outspent significantly during a campaign by our opponents, and our messages would be drowned out by their ads. But we had a clear open window prior to the election call, subject only to our available cash resources.

I had recruited for the campaign John Bowen and Eric Bell of the advertising agency Bowen and Binstock. These two were some of the best at taking research findings and translating them into communications materials. I asked them to produce a print ad and a radio ad attacking the Liberals for the anticipated early election call. I also asked for suggestions for an inexpensive media plan.

Our radio ad had a Liberal operative boasting of how this early summer election call would catch everyone napping at the cottage. We posed the question of why would they call an early $30 million election.

The print ad was brilliant. It showed a fish wrapped up in a newspaper with the message, "The Liberals are about to call an early $30-million election. You should ask why."

The tougher part was to find an inexpensive way to get out that message. Any media buy to reach a reasonable number of people would be costly and beyond our budget. We decided on a two-pronged approach. First, we would buy a very limited amount of radio across the province and a one-quarter-page ad in the *Globe and Mail* for approximately $6,000. Second, we would attempt to earn a significant amount of unpaid media by staging an event.

We convened a Friday meeting in Toronto with all of our candidates and their campaign managers, and presented the ads to them with the Queen's Park media present. The reporters were impressed. They did not expect this from us, and they liked the humour in the ads.

Over the next few days we received about $1 million worth of unpaid advertising. Our ads were played in the newscasts across the province over the weekend.

As promised, we bought the space in the *Globe and Mail* and made the small radio buy. Those ads put us on the right foot. Our candidates realized we were in the game. The media realized we were not dead. And, most important, these ads and their message set the discussion framework for the entire election. We had set the ballot box question for the election.

David Peterson called the election on the following Monday for September 6, 1990.

Our ads helped frame the question why it was necessary to be having this election so early. Even during the last week of the campaign, Peterson was being asked why he was spending $30 million on an election instead of on extra classrooms to replace portables or on extra hospital beds to improve health care.

Harris did what he said he would do. This 2000 photo shows me with Ontario premier Mike Harris. On the right is my son Brett, who worked in Harris's office from 1995 to 2000.

On September 6, Bob Rae and the NDP won a majority government, defeating David Peterson. We finished third but increased our
seat count from sixteen to twenty, and our share of the popular vote
rose from 18 percent at the start of the campaign to 23.5 percent. Mike
Harris was in a position to become premier five years later.

Low expectations had encouraged us to think outside of the box and
take risks. Doing those things, in turn, helped to ensure that we beat the
expectations people had pinned on us.

2000 FEDERAL ELECTION

A second example of managing low expectations comes from the federal
election campaign of 2000.

I had accepted Joe Clark's invitation to manage that campaign for
the PC Party of Canada. The internal and external expectations for our
campaign were extremely low — 6 percent national support is lower than
low for a national party. We had limited financial resources and would be
able to purchase only a fraction of the advertising that the Liberals and
the Canadian Alliance would buy.

Just as the election was called, we invited the Ottawa press gallery
to our headquarters for an election-preparedness briefing. As part of the
briefing we consciously attempted to deal with our low expectations and
to benefit from them.

We unveiled a print ad that we were about to place in a limited number of newspapers. It showed Prime Minister Jean Chrétien whitewater
rafting with a group of Liberals. The headline was "Jean Chrétien is about
to take you for a ride." We were not as successful at earning unpaid media
as we had been in Ontario ten years earlier, but we did show the gallery
that we were at least in the game.

At the same meeting I unveiled, in a humorous way, the travel plans
we had for the media covering the campaign. With a straight face I said
that we were unable to provide a plane, but we had made arrangements to
provide each reporter with a foot-powered scooter and a map of Canada.
I then pulled out a scooter that I had purchased for $99 and had painted

blue. The gimmick served to generate a positive feeling with the media. Again, we seemed to get off to a reasonable start by dealing up front with our low expectations.

We entered the election trailing the Liberals, the Canadian Alliance, the NDP, and even the Bloc Québécois. We continued to keep the expectations low (that was easy!) and never went off message by trying to make boastful or exaggerated claims. During the last week of the campaign, Stockwell Day, the Canadian Alliance leader, claimed that his party was going to win more than a hundred seats and was going to form the government.

On election night, Chrétien's Liberals won their third straight majority government; the Canadian Alliance came second, but won only sixty-six seats. Day was portrayed as a loser and Joe Clark was seen as

Out of the drink. This cartoon of Joe Clark shows him triumphantly riding a Sea-Doo while Stockwell Day bobs in the water behind. Stockwell Day, the new leader of the Canadian Alliance, burst onto the federal scene riding a Sea-Doo to his press conference in 2000. Day did not meet his high self-created expectations, while Clark exceeded his low expectations. Joe signed the cartoon, "To Lasch, who kept me out of troubled waters. Best wishes, Joe Clark."

a winner, despite the fact that we only won twelve seats, just enough to maintain official party status in the House of Commons, and placed fifth among the parties.

Day had failed to meet his own self-inflicted expectations, while Clark had exceeded his very low expectations. I recall having dinner with Clark two weeks later in a downtown Toronto restaurant to review the campaign and discuss the future of the party. It took him almost half an hour to leave the restaurant, as everyone wanted him to stop and talk. He was being treated like a rock star on that night, all because he exceeded expectations.

2014 TORONTO MAYORAL ELECTION

Olivia Chow's campaign for mayor of Toronto in 2014 was a classic front-runner's campaign. She was faced with the dilemma of uncontrollably high expectations. Initially, high expectations raised her up, infusing her candidacy with what would eventually turn out to be false hope. In the end, her campaign began to crater when she could not meet those high expectations and the door was left open for another candidate to walk through.

The 2014 Toronto election was unique. (I shall delve into it again in Chapter 6, on the importance of research.) The mayor since 2010 had been Rob Ford, a former Toronto city councillor, who had been elected on a promise to reduce municipal spending, to "Stop the Gravy Train," as he put it. Whatever that slogan meant, it catapulted him into office in 2010. By the midpoint of his four-year term, however, his mayoralty was in ruins. Ford had exposed himself as a drug abuser and alcoholic, given to embarrassing himself and his city by appearing in public repeatedly in what he would later describe as a "drunken stupor." By 2013 a majority of Toronto voters had turned on him, and it was clear that the mayor could be defeated by almost any sensible — and sober — candidate. It was time for a change at city hall. As 2013 wound down, two-thirds of the voters were telling the pollsters they wanted a new mayor. This number did not change significantly over the next twelve months, and on

October 27, 2014, election day, 66 percent of Torontonians voted for a candidate who was not named Ford.

For all of 2013, the public opinion polls, mainly conducted by Forum Research, showed Olivia Chow as the most credible of the potential non-Ford candidates. She enjoyed a commanding lead in the polls.

These polls included the same five potential candidates in the ballot question.

- Rob Ford — Mayor of Toronto
- Olivia Chow — NDP MP and widow of Jack Layton
- John Tory — business executive, former leader of the Ontario Progressive Conservative Party, and by 2013 a radio talk-show host in Toronto
- Karen Stintz — Toronto city councillor and chair of the Toronto Transit Commission
- David Soknacki — former city councillor and former city budget chief

During 2013, Olivia's lead over Rob Ford ranged from 3 to 17 percent in polls naming these five candidates. The race began to tighten when John Tory officially entered the race. That was on February 24, 2014.

We knew we had a challenge heading into 2014. Olivia was the leading candidate. In a choice between her and Rob Ford, she would win hands down. The polls told us that. The expectations for her were high. Way too high!

These public polls results did provide us with one large advantage. They discouraged other anti-Ford progressives from jumping into the contest. However, we sensed a larger problem could emerge at a later date because of the unrealistic expectations. Yet there was little we could do to reduce expectations. Forum Research (and some other research firms) kept publishing these numbers every month.

Focus groups results from early 2014 heightened our concerns. Voters knew very little about Olivia and her personal background. Most knew she was an NDP MP from downtown Toronto and the widow of Jack Layton. Many remembered her standing stoically by his coffin at his funeral. But they knew very little else about her. Few knew she had been a Toronto school board trustee or a Toronto city councillor and that she had a number of personal accomplishments from her previous political positions.

It became obvious that her polling numbers were being driven mainly by her high name recognition.

In an attempt to counter this situation, we decided not to run a traditional front-runner's campaign. We started the campaign aggressively on all fronts so as to not look as if we were taking the outcome for granted.

We toured aggressively. She visited forty-four wards of the city in forty-four days.

We pushed out policy planks for the first six weeks — one or two every week.

We conducted a large direct-mail fundraising campaign.

Initially, things went well. John Tory had announced his candidacy in late February with few preparations in place. After four to six weeks, our focus group respondents were saying he was invisible and they were disappointed in his passive campaign. Chow's aggressive policy statements had caught hold.

Yes, diversity matters. Olivia Chow at the 2014 Pride Parade in Toronto.

The focus groups especially liked her plans to improve bus service, to launch an after- school program for kids, and to provide help for small business.

Olivia maintained a solid lead in the public polling during April and May, the only change being that Tory had jumped into second place ahead of Rob Ford. The embattled mayor announced on May 1 that he was entering rebab for his addiction problems and would be postponing his campaign activities.

The results of the April focus groups were generally positive, although some negatives were creeping into the respondents' descriptions of my candidate. As voters were exposed to Olivia, concerns about increased spending and higher taxes began to fester. Some respondents started to comment on her difficulty in communicating in English (her second language) and her weakness at times in explaining her positions clearly. A general sense began to take hold that she was not meeting the high expectations voters had had for her.

A public poll on June 6 had Olivia with a 12 percent lead over Tory.

On June 12, the Ontario Liberal Party, led by Kathleen Wynne, not only won a majority provincial government, but they took twenty of the twenty-two seats in the city of Toronto. The New Democrats, who constituted a major part Olivia's power base, lost three of the five seats they had held in Toronto before the election. Worse, the NDP lost Trinity-Spadina, the provincial seat that coincided with her former federal constituency. It was a disaster for the NDP in Toronto, and we knew that these results would not help her mayoral campaign.

The next poll showed the first downward shift in support. Her lead over Tory dropped to 8 percent.

Then Rob Ford returned from rehab on June 30 and rejoined the campaign. The public reaction was startling. People who could not say enough critical things about him a couple of months earlier suddenly felt sympathy for him. He had been through a rough experience, but he had acknowledged his problem, sought treatment, and cleaned up his act, and now he was back asking for a second chance. We were taken aback by the number of Torontonians who were prepared to give him that second chance.

If the provincial election took some initial wind out of Chow's sails, the re-emergence of Rob Ford undermined the advantage she had enjoyed as the pre-eminent anti-Ford candidate. Suddenly, Ford, rehabilitated, was not the Darth Vader of municipal politics. He seemed to a number of people to be a stronger candidate than he had been before rehab. That unsettled the two-thirds of Torontonians who above all wanted to be rid of Ford. I began to sense the shifting mood of the public from a number of conversations with observers of the political scene and campaign volunteers. Although not everyone believed that John Tory's policies were sound (as can be seen from the *Toronto Sun* cartoon criticizing his Smart Track transit option), he seemed to have grabbed the anti-Ford mantle.

The risks in having politicians design transit plans on the back of a napkin during a campaign. Cartoon illustrating the shortcomings of John Tory's Smart Track plan.

Olivia said she was hearing the same thing on the streets from voters. She was an experienced politician, and while most Canadians tend to be kind, courteous, and gentle to political candidates whom they are not supporting, she had picked up on the shift in support.

We went into the field with a new poll of our own on July 10. The results were shocking. After leading all candidates for eighteen months, our poll had Chow trailing Tory by twelve percentage points. What had happened? In the space of just nine days there had been a net swing of twenty points against us.

What had happened? What could be done about it?

We conducted focus groups on July 21 and 22. Here is the aide-memoire I wrote at the conclusion of those groups.

> Tory is seen by many as the non-Ford candidate with momentum.
>
> Chow's strength in the downtown has been neutralized by Tory.
>
> The three policies initially proposed by Chow (improved bus service, expanded after- school programs and assistance for small business) remain very popular (as is the youth jobs plan) but most forget that they are Chow policies. Most do not know what her message is. Tory, while not seen as putting forward any policy, does receive some credit for his Smart Track transit plan.
>
> Concern about Chow raising taxes and not being a good fiscal manager continues to exist.
>
> There continues to be a desire for a pragmatic progressive mayor. Recent quantitative findings show a strong desire for investments to be made in communities and Chow is seen as the candidate most likely to make those investments. During these groups, respondents from across the city clearly say that while they like the policies proposed by Chow, they equally want a right-of-centre mayor to keep costs under control.

We never recovered from that dramatic loss in support over nine days in July. The next public poll, published on July 21, showed we were still ahead, although only by three points, but the poll after that on August 5–6 had us ten points behind Tory.

We lost the election on October 27 by 18 percent to Tory, and we trailed Doug Ford (who had taken his brother's place on the ballot after it was disclosed that Rob was entering hospital for cancer surgery) by 11 percent.

Olivia's inability to meet her high expectations had opened the door for another candidate to become the one to beat Rob Ford.

The poor provincial NDP results in Toronto started our slide in the polls. As Bob Gallagher, an experienced NDP organizer and close confidant of Olivia, commented on the situation:

> The significance of the Ontario election was not that the NDP lost, but that Toronto progressive voters voted to punish Andrea Horwath, the NDP provincial leader, for her perceived failure to articulate strong progressive positions and for not being able to present herself as the Tim Hudak [provincial PC leader] slayer. These progressives equated Horwath with Chow. Secondly, voters then made the strategic decision that Tory was the anti-Ford candidate with momentum and they moved to him.

In my view there was one other factor. Our research had continuously shown that voters wanted the next mayor to hold progressive values, but at the same time they still liked the populist "Stop the Gravy Train" message that had carried Rob Ford to victory four years previously. The voters in 2014 also decided John Tory was a safer economic alternative to the Ford boys than Olivia Chow, whom they perceived to be a free-spending socialist. Tory seemed to be progressive enough for their liking.

2015 FEDERAL ELECTION

From my point of view there were two major factors responsible for the election of Justin Trudeau and the Liberal Party of Canada on October 19, 2015. The first was the incredibly high level of desire for change. The second factor was that Trudeau significantly exceeded the low expectations that existed for him at the start of the the official campaign period on August 2, 2015.

For much of 2014 and the early part of 2015, Trudeau and the Liberals were leading in the polls. A negative television ad — "Just Not Ready" — was produced by the Conservative Party to attack Trudeau. It aired repeatedly, beginning in May. It was so effective in reducing Trudeau's voter support that the Liberals entered the formal campaign in August trailing both the NDP and the Tories in most polls, after having led or been tied for first for most of the previous twenty-four months.

The first opportunity that Trudeau had to be exposed to a large number of Canadians during the campaign was the initial televised debate with the other leaders on August 6. It was sponsored by *Maclean's* magazine. Inexplicably, on August 4, the Conservative spokesperson, Kory Teneycke, tried to put down Trudeau by telling the media that he would win debating points "if he comes on stage with his pants on." This contemptuous remark only served to draw attention to Trudeau's low expectations. The Liberal leader responded by more than holding his own during the debate.

A moment occurred during the debate that appeared to some to be the beginning of the rise of the Trudeau campaign. During a discussion of Canada's Clarity Act, Trudeau had used a question to attack the NDP's Thomas Mulcair for his opposition to the act with its requirement for a clear majority in any referendum on separation. Mulcair's position was that a simple majority — just one vote — was good enough.

Mulcair decided to pounce. He said that Trudeau needed to come clean with Canadians and tell them what number was needed for a majority to count in a referendum.

"What is your number, Mr. Trudeau?"

Trudeau started to bob and weave. "I don't question your patriotism, Mr. Mulcair …"

Mulcair asked again: "What is your number, Mr. Trudeau?"

Trudeau: "The question is …"

Mulcair asked again: "What is your number, Mr. Trudeau?"

Trudeau stopped bobbing and weaving: "You want a number, Mr. Mulcair? My number is nine."

He continued: "Nine Supreme Court Justices said that one vote is not enough to break up this country, and yet that is Mr. Mulcair's position. He wants to be the prime minister of this country and he's choosing to side with the separatist movement in Quebec and not with the Supreme Court of Canada."

It was the right answer at the right time.

The second debate was held on September 17, and again Trudeau was seen to hold his own with, and perhaps be even better than, the other leaders, thereby again exceeding voters' low expectations. Three debates were held in late September and early October, and after each of those debates the Liberals' support increased, and once again they were leading in the polls.

In staking their entire campaign on the "Just Not Ready" attack on Trudeau, the Conservatives made two critical errors. First, they lowered the expectations that voters had of Trudeau — that he was a green, light-weight, gaffe-prone politician without much substance — and second, they banked everything on Trudeau performing like that during the campaign.

By lowering expectations, the Conservatives made it relatively easy for Trudeau to not only meet but exceed those expectations. By the end of the first debate he was already being perceived as a winner. And when he continued to perform well during the long campaign, he destroyed the Conservative attack line. Harper and the Conservatives had nothing to fall back on. While the ad attempted to give voters a reason to not vote Liberal, it did not provide a reason for them to vote Conservative. In retrospect, a better attack line for the Conservatives would have been the same line used by the Liberals in 1979 against Joe Clark. During that campaign, the Liberals claimed that being prime minister was "no time for on-the-job training."

This attack would have been difficult for Trudeau to counter effectively during the campaign. Additionally, it would have provided a platform for the Conservatives from which they could have emphasized the experience of Stephen Harper, something that seemed to get lost during the election.

Ten days prior to the election I sent an email to Gerald Butts, principal adviser to Justin Trudeau. I had become convinced by the Nanos Research nightly numbers (discussed in Chapter 6) and other findings concerning time-for-a-change and the softness of the NDP vote that the Liberals would probably win a majority government. I jokingly suggested that the four actors in the Conservatives' "Just Not Ready" attack ad should be invited to Justin Trudeau's swearing in as prime minister: they had played a pivotal role in determining the outcome of the 2015 federal election. Ever the political animal, Butts suggested that it was too early to count his chickens — but they clucked loudly for him and Justin on election night.

Meeting expectations is a good start for a candidate, but exceeding expectations is a winning formula.

In the end, the fate of the campaign will be determined by the candidate himself or herself — by the effort the candidate invests in his or her candidacy, by the candidate's success in attracting capable people to work in the campaign, and by the candidate's ability to connect with his or her electorate.

The next two chapters will focus on the candidate. What steps does a prospective candidate need to take to prepare for a campaign? The answer is not as simple as you may think. The would-be politician must look in the mirror. Is she really ready to put her name on the ballot? Is he really willing to make the adjustments and sacrifices that the next weeks and months will require? The following chapter will address the importance of the homework that all candidates, regardless of gender, should complete before setting out on the rocky road to an election. The chapter after that will look at the special obstacles that lie in wait for female candidates.

Chapter 3

Preparing the Candidate

A Scout is never taken by surprise; he knows exactly what
to do when anything unexpected happens.
— LORD ROBERT BADEN-POWELL,
founder of the Boy Scouts movement

The Scout motto is "Be Prepared," which means one should always be in a state of readiness in mind and body to do one's duty. From my experience over the years, few candidates who put their names on a ballot have really heeded the motto of the Boy Scouts and Girl Guides. Few have done the homework required for their new career.

One might realistically expect that anyone getting into politics or moving up the ladder to a more senior role (including leadership) would have dedicated the time and effort to develop the personal networks and the communications skills he or she will need for the future. But too many would-be politicians assume that because politics is a game or a pursuit that is open to all, they do not need to worry about getting prepared until they actually jump onto the playing field. They should do their homework, concentrating on my simple definition of politics: people and communications.

PEOPLE

To build an organization, candidates require, as a starting point, an inventory of people who are, or could be, prepared to support them — by working on their campaign team, by contributing or raising money, or by simply undertaking to vote for them. Once an initial inventory has been compiled, a prospective candidate needs to assess the weaknesses of his or her network and create a plan to fill the gaps. This may entail reaching out to community groups, soliciting the endorsement of caucus members or other party luminaries, and enlisting the support of business leaders who will organize fundraising.

On more than one occasion I have received an uncomfortable look from new clients when I asked for their lists of supporters. While they may have names in mind or written on scattered lists, few have assembled the names in one place with potential roles indicated for each supporter.

The inventory can be compiled from a number of sources: holiday card lists, membership lists from groups the prospective candidate belongs to — Rotary, Kiwanis, Board of Trade, church, volunteer groups, neighbourhood associations, condo residents, business associates, cottagers' associations, as well as any list of people who have been financial supporters of a cause or a political party in which the client has been involved. In recent years, the inventory can be increased by the candidate's exposure to, and participation in, social-media networks — friends from Facebook, connections from LinkedIn and followers from Twitter, to name a few of the main ones.

In my experience, candidates who assemble such lists on their own initiative are rare birds. It takes effort and discipline to gather this information on a systematic basis. It is not glamorous work. You could call it grunt work. But it is work that can spell the difference between success and failure.

As the director of Belinda Stronach's campaign for the leadership of the newly constituted Conservative Party in 2004, I found myself up against Stephen Harper. Belinda had been given some credit for helping persuade Harper, then leader of the radical right Canadian Alliance, and Peter MacKay, leader of the centre-right Progressive Conservatives, to merge their parties into a new Conservative Party. But Belinda felt that neither of the two was as well suited as she was to be leader of a new party. She was young, vigorous, and full of fresh ideas. She represented the future. They were products of the political wars of the past. She believed a new party needed a new direction, new energy, and a new leader.

Others encouraged Belinda to run. One was an old client and friend of mine, Mike Harris, the former premier of Ontario, who approached me to run her campaign. She called, and in early January 2004 she came to Toronto to meet me in the boardroom of Northstar Research Partners, where I hang my hat. She told me why she wanted to run and said she had been talking to a number of people. Most had told her she would have a very steep mountain to climb. She looked at me directly and said, "I want you to help me climb that mountain."

She made Harper's climb harder. Pamphlet for Belinda Stronach's campaign for the leadership of the Conservative Party in 2004.

Harper was a formidable opponent. In part this was because, as leader of the Canadian Alliance, he had access to its membership lists to use in preparing his campaign. We did not, and it was some time before the new Conservative Party made its membership lists available to us. By the time we could contact these members Harper had out-organized and outgunned us on the ground. Belinda did come second, ahead of the third candidate, Tony Clement, a former Ontario Cabinet minister. She won 35 percent of the delegate votes, but Harper received 55 percent and became the new leader. I am not suggesting Belinda would have beaten Harper if she had his advantage of advance preparation. But she could have given him a more equal fight. She could have made his mountain a steeper climb.

We did have the benefit of some lists during that campaign. Belinda's father, Frank Stronach, was the founder and CEO of the auto-parts giant, Magna International, one of Canada's premier business success stories, and he was wholly supportive of Belinda's venture into politics. Frank had once sought a seat in the House of Commons with the underlying objective of eventually running to be leader and prime minister. He had tripped over the first step of that journey when he was defeated in his bid to become an MP. I knew he would be proud if Belinda could achieve the electoral success that had eluded him years before.

Although Frank was very respectful of my role as campaign director and seldom interfered, he did offer his help midway through the leadership campaign. Harper supporters in the national party hierarchy had approved a request from the Conservative association in Newmarket-Aurora, Belinda's federal riding, to schedule a nomination meeting. This would force Belinda to fight a local nomination contest at the same time as she was waging a national leadership campaign. The Harperites found a right-to-life Christian female candidate to contest the Newmarket-Aurora nomination. She was Harper's perfect anti-Belinda candidate.

Frank called me two or three weeks before the nomination meeting and said he was concerned. He did not want Belinda to trip over this hazard on what he saw as her journey to 24 Sussex Drive. He told me he had lists that might be useful. He wanted to check with me to see if he should use the lists of Magna employees to sell Conservative Party memberships for the local nomination meeting. I said yes, but added tongue-in-cheek that he should not send out the membership application forms with the employee pay stubs. With the influx of Magna employees, Belinda narrowly won the nomination, again demonstrating the value of being prepared.

A second and more recent example of the value of being prepared came in the 2014 Olivia Chow Toronto mayoral campaign. Olivia had never met a list she did not like or want. With the launch of her campaign, we had access to lists of tens of thousands of progressive voters in Toronto, including those with a history of making political donations. While she lost the campaign, the financial support of these progressives enabled her to finish with a small surplus after a campaign in which she raised and spent $2 million. Unlike many losing candidates, she did not have to lose financially. The value of the homework done by the accumulation of lists over many campaigns was evident in the final accounting. Gord Muschett, CEO of The Donnee Group, specialists in direct-response fundraising, said this of Olivia's campaign: "The number one key to the success was the large number of available email lists at the start of the campaign and, secondly, the volume of requests that were made to those lists during the campaign."

COMMUNICATIONS

The importance of effective communications in politics and life is obvious to most people. The specific skills required in political communications are:

- Connecting with people one-on-one
- Presenting a prepared speech
- Communicating with voters using mass media: print, radio, television, and social media
- Dressing for success

- Understanding the most effective messaging to motivate voters
- In today's multicultural Canada, achieving proficiency in a second language

And yet while the need for effective communications is obvious, few candidates I have encountered have invested much time and effort to improving their communications abilities in advance of entering public life or competing for a more senior role in elective politics.

One memorable exception was Robert Stanfield. As the relatively new leader of the PC Party of Canada he had lost the 1968 Canadian election to Pierre Trudeau. Stanfield had taken French lessons prior to that election, but he realized after losing all but two of the party's seats in Quebec that he needed to be better prepared the next time. While many gave him that advice, his encounter in 1968 with an old priest in Quebec City after a speech to a Chamber of Commerce luncheon drove home his need to improve his French. The priest approached him after his speech and said "Monsieur Stanfield, your French is very good but I can tell you that the only way that you will be able to really speak French is to have a French-speaking mistress!"

Stanfield chortled at the suggestion and went back to Ottawa to focus on his French lessons.

Shortly after the 1972 election, which he narrowly lost to Trudeau, Stanfield found himself speaking at the same Chamber of Commerce luncheon in Quebec City. After his speech, the same old priest made his way up to Stanfield and opened the conversation with a cheery greeting: "Monsieur Stanfield, who have you been sleeping with?"

While Stanfield's fluency in French improved greatly, that preparation alone was not enough to carry him to the prime minister's office in 1974.

It may seem strange that candidates would need to learn how to improve their one-on-one communications skills. After all, the impression of most voters is that politicians are natural communicators who are comfortable and adept when talking with people or, as many describe politicians, smooth talkers.

Not so fast.

Some candidates are introverts who are shy when meeting people they do not already know. Others are extroverts who lack emotional intelligence and listening skills in meetings.

I first met Premier Bill Davis in 1971 when I was asked, together with a group of other young professionals, to attend a meeting that had two objectives, one of which I learned about afterward. The first was for me and others to meet Davis and sign on as volunteers for the upcoming provincial election as advance men. The second objective was for Davis's campaign team to demonstrate to Davis that he was not very good at engaging with people he did not know. Davis was basically a shy, reserved person despite having been minister of education in the John Robarts Ontario government.

The meeting was brief. Davis came into the room where we were assembled and walked around, shook each of our hands, may have said a couple of things — and then the meeting was over. We were all so impressed at meeting a premier that it did not matter what he said. We signed on. The Davis campaign workers met with Davis after the meeting and reviewed his performance. Whatever advice they gave him, it really worked. Today, some forty-five years later, Davis continues to be one of the most effective one-on-one communicators I have encountered.

John Crosbie was another shy individual. He had to work on improving his communications skills. He took a public speaking course before entering politics. He worked hard at preparing his messages and even his sharp wit, which became a hallmark of his political career.

Some of his best exchanges were with George Baker, a Liberal MP from Newfoundland. One classic exchange involved the following quip by Crosbie: "Mr. Speaker, I am glad that the honourable gentleman finally got around to asking me this question because, if you want an answer, you have to go to the horse's mouth…. In this case, Mr. Speaker, the other end of the horse asked the question."

As a minister in the Mulroney government, Crosbie often tangled with Baker in the House of Commons. I learned later that George and John would communicate by phone from time to time in advance of the day's Question Period to review Baker's possible questions and stake out Crosbie's answers. Their homework generally paid off with great entertainment for all. That type of relationship is sorely missed at the federal level these days, as sharp personal attacks among opposing party members have become the norm.

Even candidates who are not shy in new situations may not necessarily have the skills necessary to communicate effectively with voters. While they might not have any hesitation about jumping into a conversation, few really know how to work a room. They get trapped and spend too much time with too few people.

Some candidates have difficulty maintaining eye contact as they speak to individuals one-on-one. They are diverted from the conversation at hand by the need to plan their next target in the room. By the time they move on, the last individual may be less than impressed by the exchange.

Lack of eye contact is just one barrier to effective communication. Failure to understand why nature has provided individuals with one mouth and two ears can be another barrier. Many candidates want to use those parts of their anatomy in reverse proportion. People in private life, who generally have less exciting lives than politicians, like to be able to talk and not just be talked at. The candidate who can ask a relevant question and then listen to the response will generally elicit a favourable response from a voter.

It is also an effective technique for a candidate to solicit opinions during a conversation. Many people work or live in an environment where they are mostly told what to do by their boss, banker, or spouse, and it is refreshing for them to be asked their opinion on any subject. June Rowlands, my candidate for mayor of Toronto in 1991, was one of the best candidates I have seen at engaging one-to-one with voters. She would look them in the eye and converse with them until the subject was exhausted. I cannot recall ever seeing her looking around to see whom she should talk to next.

Although this next barrier is a rare one, I remember several instances when a minor physical distraction prevented effective communication. A mole on the cheek, long eyebrows, excessive facial hair for a female, or long nostril hair for a male are prime examples of these distractions. A candidate needs to remember that what distracts will detract from the listener's ability to focus on the content of the discussion. Candidates with minor distracting characteristics need to deal with them quickly.

And, of course, lack of good personal hygiene can obliterate the effectiveness of any personal communication, whether it is bad breath or body odour. I still remember meeting a federal Liberal MP in Washington, D.C., on a Sunday evening just before she was called back to join the federal Cabinet by Prime Minister Pierre Trudeau. Her political abilities must have eclipsed her poor dental hygiene.

The reality is that many of the above barriers can be reduced or eliminated with attention or with practice.

Today the importance of personal communication pales in comparison to the need to effectively communicate with voters through the mass media. Relatively few voters will ever meet a candidate in person, and therefore most will have to rely for their impressions on what they have seen, heard, or read about a candidate through the media, including the social media.

Despite the importance of dealing effectively with the media, few candidates have taken media training to sharpen those skills. Perhaps some are deterred by the cost of such training. But it does not need to be expensive to be good. In any case, failure to learn how to communicate effectively through the media for cost reasons is being penny wise and pound foolish.

If money is indeed a significant issue, at the very least candidates should spend time watching or listening to themselves on television or radio, trying to learn about themselves. As a matter of course, I watch my candidates on television with the sound both on and off.

Dan Tisch, the CEO of Argyle PR in Toronto, is an old political friend of mine. Dan frequently trains and coaches business and political leaders, and he is one of the best that I have worked with. He is passionate about the need for politicians to develop their communications skills. He says, "Every career requires professional development, and political candidates are no different. Communications training is the ultimate investment candidates must make in themselves."

He goes on to say, "Training is a chance for a candidate to practise delivery at three levels — the visual, the tone, and the message — all done in a safe environment in the company of only trusted advisers and independent professionals."

I have seen results of studies that report that 97 percent of the communication conveyed and retained on television is visual, and only 3 percent is audio or content.

Every political candidate can remember meeting voters or friends who have seen the candidate on television and say, "I saw you on TV last night. You looked really good." Relatively few say something like, "I thought your position on free trade last night was outstanding and insightful."

However, Dan reports seeing other studies that report that tone is most important, especially in crisis situations. And, while he agrees that content is often secondary to visuals and tone, the big exception is when the content is controversial. He uses the example of Alberta Premier Jim Prentice, who told Albertans in the 2015 election to "look in the mirror." Prentice was perceived to be blaming Albertans for the province's financial situation. This message helped ensure the defeat of the Alberta PC Party.

Regardless of whether tone, visuals, or message is most important, political candidates need to invest the time to improve all aspects of their communications.

I think of candidates who spend countless hours working on a text for a speech and precious few minutes practising their delivery. Sometimes they are better off not giving the speech at all. Voters' takeaways will be based mainly on their impression of what they see. Did the candidate look comfortable in his or her skin? Was the candidate angry? Composed? Calm? Under control? Energetic? Did the speaker look interested?

Another aspect of candidate communication is personal dress. There are lots of books written by professionals that provide advice on "how to dress for success." It is not my intention to provide those details in this chapter. However, I will say again that few candidates ever take the time to prepare themselves for this next step in their lives.

Canadians generally want their politicians to look a little better dressed than the average person. However, they do not want them to be dressed over the top. Politicians in recent years have taken to wearing jeans and sport shirts to establish a relationship with the middle class. It is very likely that the clothes for this casual, dressed-down look are quality garments, purchased at Holt Renfrew, not Walmart. White shirts and blue suits are reserved for dress-up occasions such as a major speech at a Board of Trade luncheon.

Perhaps candidates have other things on their minds than clothes as they get ready for an election, but I have had a number of male clients who have been totally unprepared for this aspect of a campaign. I do not regard myself a fashion plate, and I am not one, as my wife will verify, but I do know which clothes are made from quality fabrics and which are not, which colours are not in, what a too-loud check is — and what a well-worn suit and a frayed shirt collar look like. On a number of occasions, my first meeting with a candidate has included a visit to a bedroom. I go through the clothes closet and wardrobes with ruthless dispatch. When I'm done the keepers are on the bed. The discards are on the floor. This is a humiliating experience for most candidates, as the floor pile is always significantly higher than the one on the bed.

I recall my first meeting with Tom Rideout in his office at the House of Assembly in St. John's in 1989. He wanted to run for the leadership of the PC Party of Newfoundland and Labrador. During that meeting I took away his package of cigarettes. I told him that if he really wanted to win he should stop smoking, because voters, especially younger ones, tend to think that a politician who smokes cannot be very bright. The next afternoon I did my clothes inventory with him in his bedroom, with predictable results. He did not have much left to campaign in.

His wife, Jacinta, whom I had just met, came into the bedroom and surveyed the pile on the floor. I could tell she was not happy. She looked me straight in the eye and said, "I don't care what you tell Tom to do. But let's get this straight, I am not giving up smoking."

I sadly remembered this exchange fourteen years later when I learned of Jacinta's passing from lung cancer.

Having said the message is less important than the presentation, I must qualify that by noting candidates do need a message to be effective at motivating voters. To be effective, the message or content needs to be relevant and credible, even inspirational.

One part of the process an individual goes through in deciding to become a candidate should include an answer to the question that will be asked sooner or later: "Why do you want to be leader, MP, MPP, or mayor?"

This question may give a candidate his or her first clear opportunity to motivate the voters. And yet, from my experience, only a few very good candidates have prepared a response in advance. The good candidates have rehearsed it — and they feel it.

Ed Goeas, president and CEO of the Tarrance Group, a U.S. political research firm, played a leading role in the elections of two governors who became potential Republican presidential nominees for 2016 — Scott Walker of Wisconsin and John Kasich of Ohio. Goeas captures the need to understand what turns a voter's crank with the following observation: "All political communication occurs in the mind of the listener, not out of the mouth of the candidate."

Candidates need to understand the values that are important to voters in order to be able to connect with, and motivate, their voters. In Chapter 7, where I discuss vision, policy, and values, I will describe my version of the list of values that are important to most Canadians. Each candidate needs to create his or her own list. Each needs to understand which values he or she can genuinely buy into, and then proceed to formulate policies and messaging that convey those values to the voters. Focus group research can be a valuable tool to provide insights into the thinking of voters.

I recently read an op-ed by David Brooks in *The New York Times* entitled "The Moral Bucket List." He described his assessment of all the "good" people he had met in his life — those "who radiated an inner light" — and he came to the conclusion that good people are made and not born. They prepare themselves.

He observed that each person has two sets of virtues or, as I call them, values. These are the resumé virtues and the eulogy virtues.

The résumé virtues are the skills that each person brings to the marketplace, and these virtues are what most people work hard to develop. The eulogy virtues are the ones talked about in the eulogy delivered at your funeral — whether you were brave, honest, faithful, compassionate, or caring. Although these virtues are the more important ones, he observed that our culture and educational systems expend more time teaching life skills and resumé virtues than they do in moulding inner character.

Only outstanding politicians have taken the time to understand what values are most important to voters and then worked to make sure those values apply to themselves. This is a tough challenge. It is much more difficult than building up one's resumé with degrees at university, travel abroad, or participation as a volunteer with charities or local community groups.

An important part of the preparation to be a candidate is to demonstrate a strong desire or passion to have the job. Over the past forty years I have come to understand that this factor often comes into play in determining electoral success. Does the person standing for election appear to be prepared to work hard for the privilege of holding office?

Sadly, far too many citizens have a poor perception of politicians. I have seen research over the years ranking various professions in terms of favourability. Nurses are always at the top of the list and politicians are very near the bottom, usually just slightly ahead of rock stars and used-car salespeople. The reasons given are varied but include the perception that politicians are paid a lot of money and enjoy perks that most of us can only dream of, but do not work terribly hard at the job.

One silver lining for currently elected politicians is the research finding that while voters do not have a positive impression of politicians in general, they usually have a more favourable impression of their local elected representatives. That, coupled with a higher level of name recognition, means incumbents generally tend to be re-elected — in the absence of dramatic events or a high level of unfavourability tied to a particular event or action.

For most voters, a politician who is out of sight is a politician who is not working on their behalf. If they do not see or hear from their representative, their negative perceptions take over and they assume the worst.

Tip O'Neill, the well-known former speaker of the U.S. Senate, is known for his comment "All politics is local." This encapsulates the principle that a politician's success is directly tied to the ability to understand and influence the issues of the politician's constituents. Voters often feel that candidates cannot do this unless they are visible to the voter and can be seen working on behalf of the community. A candidate who is visibly working hard to win an election generates the perception that, once elected, he or she would work as hard on behalf of constituents. In addition, a candidate who is visible is generally perceived as being better at understanding the issues facing the community.

Two politicians who enjoyed success by branding themselves as local, aggressive, and hard-working politicians in preparation for their elections were Heward Grafftey, a Progressive Conservative MP from Quebec, and the late Rob Ford, the former mayor of Toronto. I knew them both, but I was not directly involved with their campaigns.

Heward Grafftey was an MP for eighteen years from the Quebec riding of Brome-Missisquoi. Heward kept getting elected because he had a well-deserved reputation of starting his next re-election campaign the day after each victory. He continually knocked on doors in his riding. Despite the fact that his party was soundly defeated in Quebec each time, he continued to be personally re-elected.

The second politician, Toronto Mayor Rob Ford — Jimmy Kimmel's favourite Canadian politician — I first encountered in 2010. By the time Ford had entered the mayoral campaign that year he had a well-defined brand image of being fiscally prudent and, more important, of personally returning every phone call from his constituents. This claim to fame was generated during his ten years as a city councillor. His was the brand image of a man who was in touch with the people. That was the major reason why he became the sixty-fourth mayor of Toronto that year.

Although Ford's term as mayor was marked by a series of scandals, including his drug use, his reputation as a fighter for "the little guy" remained strong amongst a large segment of the voting population, especially those dubbed "Ford Nation." As Marcus Gee of the *Globe and Mail* said after Ford's passing in 2016, "He was able to forge an extraordinary bond with many ordinary people."

Over the years, different politicians have used varying techniques to demonstrate that they want the job in advance of an election. I offer the following for consideration by people who are considering applying for elected public office:

- In this era of high technology, use the technology to follow the example of Heward Grafftey and keep in personal touch with the voters. It takes some short-term pain but can provide long-term gain.
- Aggressively assume a position in support of a local issue that is important, or should be important, to your community.
- Develop an aggressive visual-media strategy designed to show voters that work is being done by you on issues important to them. In this era of overflow communications, a picture (or video) is definitely worth more than a thousand words.

I have been using the word "aggressive" here. In thinking about the impact of being perceived as an aggressive candidate, I have come to believe that this trait reveals a value that most voters admire or respect — a strong work ethic.

The advantage of being aggressive was demonstrated by Justin Trudeau and the Liberals in the lead-up to the 2015 federal campaign. In March 2012, MP Trudeau had accepted a challenge to fight Conservative Senator Patrick Brazeau in a charity boxing match. Brazeau, with military and martial arts training, was heavily favoured to win. Trudeau, who had been taught to defend himself by his father, won the fight with a TKO. Trudeau appeared to have taken a big chance and won big politically. The entire nation got to witness his victory via the mass media and Internet.

I recently learned that Justin may not have left the outcome of this fight entirely to chance. He apparently trained extensively in a gym for almost six months. Regardless of the level of risk he undertook, Trudeau beat expectations and won big politically with this event.

This carried through into the campaign, as the Liberals presented their leader in interesting and different visuals as he was preparing for the all-party leader debates. These images demonstrated that Trudeau was aggressively seeking the job of prime minister. Whether it was paddling a canoe or going a few rounds with his boxing sparring partner, Trudeau was perceived to be "on his toes" and not settling back and being comfortable.

The new champ: an early example of exceeding expectations. Justin Trudeau wins charity boxing match against heavily favoured Conservative Senator Patrick Brazeau in 2012.

Improving one-on-one communication skills, collecting the largest lists, improving presentation skills, improving language proficiency, acquiring an appropriate wardrobe, and having solid eulogy virtues cannot guarantee political success, but in all my experiences, few candidates have made it to the finish line without a certain level of completed homework.

The lessons and observations in this chapter apply equally to male and female candidates. Female candidates, however, face unique pressures and challenges. They need to take additional steps to prepare for becoming candidates for public office. In the next chapter I will address some of these issues, including clothing, fundraising, and getting ready to deal with the old boys' club. I will also reflect on the need for leaders to do a better job than they have historically done in preparing their parties to assist women to secure nominations in winnable ridings.

Chapter 4

Preparing a Female Candidate

Because it's 2015.
— JUSTIN TRUDEAU

Justin Trudeau's dramatic appointment of a gender-equal Cabinet has shown leadership in the long, uphill battle to break through the glass ceiling in politics. While his was not the first Cabinet in Canada to have an equal number of men and women, it is certainly the most high profile government to reach that goal. In Quebec the government of Liberal Premier Jean Charest accomplished it in 2007, and in Alberta NDP Premier Rachael Notley got there in May 2015, slightly ahead of Trudeau. Trudeau, like Charest, managed it with a smaller pool of elected women than Notley had at her disposal.

Consider the numbers of female MPs, MNAs, or MLAs that these three leaders had to draw on for their Cabinet selections.

	Women as % of all elected representatives (all parties)	Women as % of elected government party representatives
Women in House of Commons, 2015	26%	27%
Women in Quebec Legislature, 2007	26%	35%
Women in Alberta Legislature, 2015	33%	47%

As long as the percentage of elected women hovers around the 25 or 26 percent level, leaders who are intent on achieving gender equality will effectively be telling their male supporters that their chance of getting into Cabinet is about one-half that of their female colleagues. The ultimate impact of this policy will be to hamstring the ability of leaders and their campaign managers to recruit highly qualified male candidates. It will be damaging to overall caucus morale. In my view, Cabinet gender equality is not sustainable as a long-term policy.

Let me hasten to clarify that statement. A policy of gender-equal Cabinets makes sense until natural or other forces bring about something approaching parity in the numbers of women and men in our legislatures. Until then, quotas or other forms of affirmative action will be required. The actions of Charest, Notley, and Trudeau were admirable because the goal is worthwhile. The goal is to reassure women who seek to have a career in public life that they will have an equal shot at advancement, and that the walls of the political old boys' club are being torn down.

Not long ago the notion of a Cabinet, federal or provincial, composed of as many women as men would have seemed absurd or impossibly idealistic. Flora MacDonald, an icon of the Red Tory movement and a champion of women in politics, recalled that in 1972, when she was first elected to Parliament for Kingston and the Islands, she became the only woman in the 107-member Progressive Conservative caucus. She found it a lonely existence: "North America has been appallingly slow to accept women as the equals of men in public life," she commented a few years before her death in 2015.

> I was accustomed to being the only woman in a man's world. It was like that during the years when for all practical purposes I was running Conservative headquarters, when I was the first woman admitted to the National Defence College in Kingston, and when, after the 1972 election, I was the only woman in the Progressive Conservative caucus. Our society reserves special scrutiny for ambitious females trying to climb the political ladder in a system

that is male-oriented and male-dominated and whose
rules are written by men.

Although things have changed since MacDonald's day, progress
up that political ladder continues to be painfully slow. A record
eighty-eight women were elected to Parliament in October 2015. But
they represented just 26 percent of members elected — an increase
of a scant 1 percent since the previous election in 2011. According
to the statistics compiled by the Inter-Parliamentary Union, Canada
currently ranks 61st of 191 countries in the proportion of elected
female politicians at the national level.

To Victoria Budson, the founding executive director of the Women
and Public Policy Program at Harvard University, the argument for
having more women in elected office is a practical one: representative
governments work better when they can draw on the life experiences of
women as well as men. "We need a Congress that mirrors the experiences
of the citizenry — not just for equality, but for effectiveness," she says.

Fifteen years ago, a group of Canadian women met to create an organization that would advocate for improved numbers of women at the
federal and provincial levels of government. Donna Dasko, whose house
was the site of the first meeting, became one of the co-founders of Equal
Voice and, later, national co-chair.

Donna does not see having more women as a practical matter, but
rather one of creating a stronger and fairer democracy. She goes on to
say, "As a pollster, I know that women tend to have different points of
view than men on a number of key public policy issues, such as health
care, social services, the military, and others. If women are not equally
represented, their views are not adequately represented on these files."

It can be argued that Rachel Notley had an easier job in selecting her
gender-equal Cabinet than either Charest or Trudeau because she had an
almost the same number of women as men in her caucus following the
2015 Alberta election. However, she had done the hard work up front by
ensuring that the NDP nominated as many female as male candidates.
Notley had not committed to a specific number, but she did promise
to have a high percentage of female candidates. The final percentage of

female NDP candidates was 53 percent, and women accounted for 47 percent of her elected caucus.

Like Notley, Justin Trudeau did not set a target for the number of female candidates he wanted. But the Liberal Party did have a rule that in order for a nomination meeting to proceed, the riding association had to have conducted an acceptable search for contestants, including documented evidence of a thorough search for potential candidates who were female and who were reflective of the demographic and linguistic makeup of the local electorate. (Even so, only 31 percent of Liberal candidates in 2015 were women.)

Most political parties in Canada have adopted measures to attract and support female candidates. These include special funds to help nominated women cover their campaign-related costs. The New Democratic Party, which has historically attracted more female candidates than the other parties, has a long-standing policy of freezing nominations until riding associations can demonstrate that a genuine search has been made for women or other candidates from under-represented groups. Overall, however, the default position for most parties is to nominate males in the absence of nomination rules, guidelines, or quotas suggesting preferential treatment or consideration for women.

Although trailing badly behind the Scandinavian countries in particular, Canada is doing better than some democracies, and about the same as others, in terms of the number of elected female representatives both at the federal level (26 percent as of 2016) and provincial level (28 percent). The latest national figure for India is 12 percent. And in the United Kingdom women make up 29 percent of legislators. In Washington, women make up 20 percent of the membership of the Senate and 19 percent of the House of Representatives.

According to the most recently available statistics (from 2013), the world average in democratic nations is 21 percent female parliamentarians. These national numbers suggest to me the existence of a glass ceiling somewhere between 25 and 30 percent.

Currently, females represent 26 percent of the elected provincial parliaments, and three provinces lead the way — British Columbia (37.6

percent), Ontario (35.5 percent), and Alberta (33.3 percent). Is it just a coincidence that these three provinces have female premiers?

I have had the pleasure of managing or being the strategist for eight female candidates — 16 percent of my campaigns over the last forty-plus years. I have also worked with many very talented women in the back-rooms of all of my campaign organizations. On a number of occasions some of these women have taken the skills learned and networks developed in my campaigns to run their own campaigns for elected office. These include Kathy Dunderdale, the former premier of Newfoundland and Labrador; Janet Ecker, former minister of finance in Ontario; Alison Redford, former premier of Alberta; and Jennifer Hollett, an NDP Toronto candidate in the 2015 federal election.

While political parties have taken some steps to improve the odds for women, and while organizations such as Equal Voice have done much to draw public attention to the issue and to provide programs and resources for female candidates, my experience over the years has been that women still face some very significant barriers. These will not be easily overcome without bold actions in the backrooms of politics that correspond to those taken by Charest, Notley, and Trudeau in the front rooms.

THE BARRIERS WOMEN FACE

The barriers encountered by women are both societal and financial. Perhaps the largest barrier is that many women already have two or three jobs and cannot see how they can manage another. It is well recognized that females are usually the primary caregiver in the family unit. They are the quarterbacks in the family in dealing with the health, education, and community needs of their parents, their children, themselves, and often their male spouse as well.

During the Olivia Chow mayoral campaign in Toronto (which I discuss in Chapters 2, 6, and 8) I saw firsthand the challenges that a woman has to face with family issues. Recently widowed, Olivia had her father in a nursing home, and she faced the ongoing demands of that situation — visiting him, meeting with doctors and caregivers to review his condition, and arranging for home visits. She also had her elderly mother living at home with her. Arranging for regular care, taking her to dental and medical appointments, and the normal day-to-day attention she required took much of Olivia's time and attention. Her mother fell three times during the campaign, injuring ribs and wrists. I cannot think of many male candidates who have had to bear responsibility for personally dealing with these types of family issues during a pressure-filled campaign.

Another barrier female candidates must surmount is the lack of comfort that many women experience in the political theatre. The media portrayal of politics as a rough-and-tumble sport does little to encourage women to become candidates. The gruelling demands of an election campaign and the follow-up demands, if elected, are also not a positive motivation for most women. The personal acrimony among politicians, which seems to have increased significantly in recent years, has almost certainly reduced the inclination of many women and men to enter politics.

Then there is the sexist attitude, or old boys' club, as Flora MacDonald experienced it, and its impact upon women's inclination to get into politics. The "OB club," while arguably smaller and less influential than it used to be, still exists. It still discourages many competent women from venturing into a career in politics.

I remember the 1970s controversy over allowing women to become members of the Albany Club, the bastion of Conservatism in Toronto. Ontario Premier Bill Davis had made provincial history in 1971 by appointing two women to his Cabinet: Margaret Scrivener and Margaret Birch. He decided he also wanted to nominate both of them for membership in the Albany Club. The membership committee of the club did not know what to do when the nomination papers arrived: women were allowed to attend events at the club but were not permitted to be members. Davis asked Attorney General Roy McMurtry to second the nomination of each woman. After much dithering and delay, the fearless membership committee decided to pass the buck; it would put the question to a referendum of club members. The vote allowing female members passed, but to the surprise of many in the club it was the older members who voted yes, while younger members opposed the change.

Astute women have found ways to disarm hidebound old boys' clubs. Jean Pigott, the CEO of Morrison Lamothe Bakery, a large food manufacturer in Ottawa, told me how she handled one such situation. When she was appointed to the board of directors of Ontario Hydro by Premier Davis, she was the first non-engineer ever to serve on the board. Davis had wanted her to bring retail skills and sensitivities to the deliberations of the board. When she attended her first board meeting, she took cookies made by her firm to distribute. After I helped her get elected as a Progressive Conservative MP in a 1976 by-election in Ottawa-Carleton, I watched her use the same technique successfully with the overwhelmingly male Tory caucus. The simple act of offering cookies to her male colleagues allowed her to break the ice with them and let them understand that she was bringing a different approach to the game.

Last, but not least, among the barriers women must face is the money barrier. As a general proposition, few women who are considering a political future have developed a network of individuals who could be significant financial supporters for their election campaigns. They are also daunted by the amount of money that is required and by the war stories they hear about candidates being left with huge debts when the campaign is over.

Patty Hajdu, appointed by Justin Trudeau as the federal minister of status of women, described her "intense fear" of raising money for her political campaign. "I think there is probably a gender difference there. I didn't have any trouble asking people to donate to the homeless shelter (the organization that she headed) — that was always just fine. But to ask people to donate money so that I could win an election felt really awkward."

Ms. Hajdu addressed her fear by networking. She found three experienced fundraisers in her community who helped her.

Women should know that the Internet can also help address financial concerns about entering politics. I am not saying that raising money will ever be easy, but these tools can help in developing networks that can substitute for the personal financial networks that are readily available to many males. With the assistance of lists accumulated over a number of campaigns, the Olivia Chow campaign succeeded in raising more than 60 percent of its total $2 million budget in online contributions. Olivia finished third but exited the campaign debt-free.

* * *

There may also be a broader societal issue at play here. In 2008, the Brookings Institution in the United States released the results of research they had conducted with their Citizen Political Ambition Panel over a number of years. They found that more men than women have political ambition. They attributed the persistent gender gap in political ambition to several factors, many of which I have described above. They offered an additional reason. They reported that women are less likely to think that they are "qualified" for public office. While I have not seen that myself, you have to remember that I have been dealing mainly with women who have already decided to be candidates or senior campaign officials.

Other research from the Center for American Women in Politics may help to partially explain this difference in political ambition or motivation. In a survey of both elected male and female state legislators who were asked for the number one reason why they first ran for office, men were more likely to say that they had a long-standing interest in politics and a political career. Women reported that they became involved because of a public policy issue. Debbie Walsh, the director of the Center, said tellingly, "Our shorthand for this is that women run to do something and men run to be somebody."

On the positive side of this issue, the Brookings Institution reports that extensive research shows that when women do run for office they perform just as well as men. The research concludes that a major part of the solution to gender equity in politics is to ensure that more women get recruited; more information about the electoral environment and the use of female mentors can encourage women to offer themselves as candidates.

SOME DISADVANTAGES FOR WOMEN — AND SOME ADVANTAGES

There are some disadvantages that women face that I have seen first-hand. There is a double standard with respect to being aggressive if the candidate is female. While aggressive men are applauded by the media and voters, women who are aggressive are portrayed as domineering or ambitious.

The double standard extends well beyond that. I watched as my candidate, Belinda Stronach, was lampooned by the media for using a homespun example of how she would approach jobs, taxes, and the economy when she ran against Stephen Harper and Tony Clement for the leadership of the newly formed Conservative Party in 2004. She said she would focus on making a larger pie so that there would be more for everyone. I doubt that Harper or Clement would have been mocked so mercilessly had either used the same analogy. Nor would their privacy have been invaded or their personal lives dissected the way Stronach's was by the national media during that ultimately doomed campaign. She was portrayed as being too rich, too good looking, and too politically inexperienced to be taken seriously. Neither of her male opponents had those perceptions to overcome.

From my experiences, I would add that much more needs to be done to improve the safety and comfort of the political environment in order to attract more women to politics. Many women have an aversion to extremely competitive environments. An effort to increase the civility of politics and to make the world of an elected representative more female-friendly would help. Some governments have reduced the number of evening sittings of their parliaments. Some have set out a calendar of parliamentary votes one year in advance. Votes are held mainly during the day in the middle of each week to provide women with additional comfort and flexibility in dealing with their challenging and hectic personal environment.

Prime Minister Justin Trudeau has instructed his House Leader, Dominic LeBlanc, to review various aspects of Parliament with a view to making the House of Commons a more female-friendly and family-friendly environment.

Other legislatures in Canada have taken up the same review. Alberta had to face the issue when it came to light that an MLA who was about to give birth would have her pay docked if she missed more than ten sitting days.

Nancy Peckford of Equal Voice says that so much more needs to be done to encourage women to run for office. She says, "While the structural/institutional realities are often a significant disincentive for women, it's the culture of politics that is equally demotivating."

I support the observation by the Brookings Institution that once women become candidates they generally do as well as men. In my experience, female candidates actually enjoy some significant advantages over their male counterparts during elections. This starts right from an analysis of the demographics of the electorate. There are generally 8 percent more females than males in the voting population. While women do not vote as a bloc, female candidates should have, and can have, an advantage with female voters by better understanding their issues and concerns. Female candidates tend to be more sensitive to social issues (health care, education, and care for seniors) that impact all voters, but especially female voters.

I have observed that generally women are better at developing and working networks than men. Women usually have no problem with asking for help from men and women. They do it naturally as part of a learning process. Men seem less inclined to ask for help because it could be seen as a sign of weakness on their part, just as many male drivers refuse to stop and ask for directions when they get lost.

Politics is all about relationships (people and communications) and, again from my viewpoint, women are generally better at forging and maintaining relationships than men. It seems to be in their nature to be better communicators than men and generally to be better listeners.

A significant advantage for female candidates is the number of former elected politicians who are willing, if asked, to be mentors for female candidates. These individuals are also ready to help men, but women tend to be more likely to ask them for help.

I might note that former politicians are not the only individuals who welcome being asked for their opinions and assistance. I can recall discussions from many focus groups where participants told me they have little control over their lives. Their bosses, spouses, lawyers, accountants, and lovers, not to mention the rules of society, told them what to do and when to do it. How refreshing it is for many when someone asks them for help or for their opinion. They generally respond positively.

Women also enjoy an advantage over men when it comes to dressing for politics. Men have limited options: traditionally, a blue suit, a white or blue dress shirt, and a necktie that is not too flamboyant; more recently, a business-casual outfit of denim shirt, sports jacket, and jeans. As of the 2015 federal election, men have been liberated to the extent that it is now acceptable to appear in public in colourful patterned socks, thanks to Justin Trudeau.

Women have a wide range of colours to work with in their choice of outfits to get noticed. My advice to female candidates is to stick to solid colours and avoid patterns and frills. Solid colours — red, blue, yellow, and green — are most visible in a room or on a stage. They also project stability and strengths, virtues that voters seek in candidates.

That said, female candidates have to work much harder than men in dressing for each campaign day. Unlike men, who might only need to change their tie, or take it off, to look different, women generally need three or four outfits for each day. The public doesn't expect a female candidate to show up in the same outfit for a radio interview, a breakfast fundraiser, a luncheon speech to a chamber of commerce audience, door-to-door canvassing, or an all-candidates debate. I should note that regardless of gender, candidates need to consider their campaign outfits as uniforms, similar to that of a professional athlete. They are meant to be worn extensively for two or three months and then are usually put in the garbage after the game on election day.

While there are advantages and disadvantages for female candidates once nominated, Donna Dasko sees the main challenge being to encourage the country's political parties to adopt policies and practices to nominate more women, especially in winnable ridings.

Donna points to the New Democratic parties at the federal and provincial levels. "They are required to seek out women and minority candidates before they schedule nomination meetings. This practice has resulted in substantially more women running for that party and more women elected to their caucuses. If other parties adopted such practices, we could see a real improvement in the numbers of women elected."

Justin Trudeau credited the political environment of 2015 as his motivation for creating a gender-equal Cabinet. The challenge that lies ahead for him, and all others in political leadership in Canada and elsewhere, will be to use that rationale to take similar bold action in the backrooms of politics. This would mean that in the future, gender-equal Cabinets will be more likely treated as the norm and not as a significant media story.

The spirit of 2015 has also swept into the media. The *Globe and Mail* has assigned veteran political columnist Jane Taber to write a regular series of articles under the banner "Women in Politics" detailing the challenges and solutions for female candidates. This again can only help the situation.

Prime Minister Trudeau has promised to change the electoral system and depending on which electoral system is chosen that could also be a game-changer for women in Canada. Dasko points out that many of the countries with much higher numbers of women in their parliaments have electoral systems with some form of proportional representation. I can only guess that members of Equal Voice will be active in the debate on changing the electoral system.

Once the candidate has been selected and prepared for battle, she — or he — will need certain weapons or tools with which to wage the combat that lies ahead. First and foremost will be the campaign organization that the candidate needs to put together, the subject of the next chapter.

Chapter 5

The Impact of Organization

Organization doesn't win elections, but it sure can lose them.
— NORMAN ATKINS, senator,
campaign manager, and advertising executive

O f course it is not just candidates who need to prepare themselves. Campaign organizers also need to work to prepare for their responsibilities.

This point was driven home to me by the late Eddie Goodman, shortly after I was appointed national director of the Progressive Conservative Party in June 1973. Although I had heard of "Fast Eddie" (as he was fondly known) prior to my appointment, I knew little about him other than that he was a Toronto lawyer who had been campaign chairman for Robert Stanfield in 1968 and was an adviser to Bill Davis. He showed up at national headquarters during my first week on the job. In five minutes he told me what I needed to do for the next five years as national director. His basic message was that because I was new to the party and the party's senior people were new to me, I needed to quickly develop a personal network of contacts across Canada that I could work with and count on. Then, like a whirling dervish, he was gone.

I realized he had given me great advice. The next morning I met with my secretary, Jean Greenfield, and, applying my IBM systems training, we developed a plan that I followed for the next few years. I had Jean put all the names of senior party personnel on four-by-six-inch index cards. We used different colours. The names on the white cards received a call from me once a week. The blue cards were called biweekly, and the green cards were called every three weeks. I kept brief notes on the conversations on the cards. I asked Jean to put five cards on my desk each morning.

Within six months I had assembled a pretty good network that assisted me greatly during my five years as national director.

Two other political organizers who influenced me greatly were Keith Davey and Norman Atkins. Liberal senator Keith Davey, known as "the Rainmaker," was the master organizer in Canada in the 1960s and 1970s. I got to know the other, Conservative senator Norman Atkins, in 1971 when he and his brother-in-law Dalton Camp were running Ontario's Big Blue Machine and I was a volunteer advance man. Norman was the master organizer in the 1970s and 1980s.

In his book *The Big Blue Machine*, J. Patrick Boyer describes how the PC Party's Big Blue Machine pioneered electoral techniques in Canada of centralized control, campaign advertising, polling, policy presentation, and fundraising. The "machine" consisted of a widespread

Group photo of team I assembled for Brian Peckford's 1979 Newfoundland and Labrador provincial election. Among those pictured are Norman Atkins (right), Nancy McLean (holding sign), and Brian Armstrong (rear). The downtown St. John's building in the background was the home of John Crosbie's mother in the early 1900s and later became a brothel. It was our base for Peckford's campaign.

yet close-knit network of organizers and specialists who changed how campaigns were fought.

As Boyer's book describes, Dalton was essentially the guru and Norman was effectively the driver of the locomotive. While many of the specialists were not well-known names, others were, including Senator Finlay MacDonald; Senator Hugh Segal; sports broadcaster Ward Cornell; Ontario Cabinet minister Roy McMurtry; John Tory, current mayor of the City of Toronto; Phil Lind, vice-chair of Rogers; Brian Armstrong, Bruce Power senior executive; and Ross Degeer, former executive director of the Ontario PC Party.

Norman's view of the impact of organization on the outcomes of elections is mostly consistent with my own. Candidates generally win or lose on their own merits or demerits. The candidate's name is on the ballot,

Organizations can't win elections, but they sure can lose them. This 1973 photo shows members of the Big Blue Machine at the black-tie dinner honouring Malcolm Wickson, who would be the PC Party's campaign manager in the 1974 national election. Malcolm (dressed as a shepherd to Stanfield's left) endorsed the photo: "John: What are two old pros doing with these amateurs?"

Let's Be the Best We Can Be. During the 1985 Ontario PC Party leadership campaigns Larry Grossman left the singing and the songs to Bruce Springsteen. "Dancing in the Dark," can't light a fire without a spark. He did provide the spark that attracted a large group of bright imaginative people who introduced many innovative campaign techniques.

not the campaign manager's or the strategist's. However, there are times in very close elections where organization can be the defining difference between success and failure, and I have seen a number of these instances "up close and personal." It is therefore important for the candidate and the campaign manager to put in the time and effort before the start of the campaign to identify and recruit the best people possible.

On a number of occasions I have been involved with campaigns where there is tremendous excitement because of the personality and/ or vision of the candidate. The two Ontario PC Party leadership campaigns of Larry Grossman in 1985 (held to replace the retiring Bill Davis) were cases in point. Each of his campaigns was remarkable, both for the large number of people, political veterans and newcomers alike, attracted to the candidate and for the innovative ideas that were introduced to politics in the areas of campaign materials, communications, and delegate management.

A thirtieth reunion party was held in 2015 and I was struck by the many individuals from those two campaigns who went on to play important roles in politics at the federal and provincial levels. A partial list includes Janet Ecker, Tony Clement, Graham Scott, Phil Gillies, Leslie Noble, Alastair Campbell, Allan Gregg, Tom Scott, Alan Schwartz, John Tory, Hugh Segal, and Jo-Anne Polak.

The Impact of Organization

Many individuals are attracted to a political campaign because of the candidate, and many of these become volunteers on the campaign team. Volunteers are free labour, but their presence dictates that campaign managers need to have another skill set in their repertoire — that of managing volunteers.

The remainder of the campaign personnel will be paid staff, and a campaign manager normally has the major role in hiring those individuals. However there will usually be close consultation with the candidate, especially for those positions that require a personal working relationship with the candidate, such as an executive assistant, media relations officer, director of communications, or social-media specialist.

While every campaign organization is unique because it is composed of different personalities and faces different challenges, each team goes through the same development process. Each starts from nothing more tangible than the candidate's dream. It grows every day and, if all goes well, the organization will be operating at peak efficiency and effectiveness on election day.

It is vital that campaign managers keep this development process in mind when planning events and other activities, especially at the start of an election. These activities should be set with realistic objectives in mind, because a brand new organization is a fragile thing. The members are strangers to each other, and most are new to the candidate. In most campaigns, none have worked together before. Failure to meet objectives at an early event, such as a campaign launch, will slow the development of the team, create poor morale, convey to all that the campaign does not know what it is doing, and, worse, will damage the confidence that the candidate has in his or her organization.

I always say that political organizations are living, breathing organisms that require nurturing in order to survive and grow successfully. That nurturing includes the building of confidence, positive reinforcement for jobs done well, and close communication to minimize the risks of early failures.

I compare the launch of a campaign to the takeoff of an airplane. It is a success if you get off the ground without hitting any trees at the end of the runway. If you plan an event for 1,000 people and only 500 show up, it is a failure. Reading Jerry Bruno's book *The Advance Man* in 1971, I was impressed by his example of how he would plan an event to mark the Second Coming of Christ. He would not hold it in Yankee Stadium with tens of thousands of people, but rather in a hall that would hold just 500 people, and have people hanging out of the doors and windows and from the rafters. He would want the media to describe the event as exceeding all expectations, with an overflow crowd of excited and enthusiastic supporters.

As the campaign progresses, other elements come into play. These include having large doses of fun and regularly scheduled social events, constantly recognizing the achievements of team members, and providing food in the campaign office.

Early on, the campaign manager needs to establish a schedule of regular meetings for the various committees that meet at all levels of the organization. The membership of some of these meetings is honorary, while others require strategic or operational personnel.

By way of example, I will use parts of a report that I was asked to provide to Don Getty and his campaign team in August 1985 for his pursuit of the Alberta Progressive Conservative leadership following the resignation of Premier Peter Lougheed. They had asked for my assistance in organizing their central campaign. My major recommendations provide a real-life example of the meetings that need to take place and their frequency and membership composition.

> The challenge over the next two or three weeks will be to accelerate the development of the central operations to be in a position to support and direct the grassroots organization.
>
> I would suggest that there be three levels of committees:
>
> - **Advisory Board** — to act as sounding board for campaign — wise old heads. This committee should meet two or three times prior to the convention. Each member should also be asked to be involved in the telephone calling of delegates where useful.
> - **Executive Committee** — to act as strategy creation

group and to provide basic operational and policy guidelines to the operations committee. Should meet weekly or as required. Candidate should attend when possible and candidate's spouse should be encouraged to attend some of the meetings. The members are there because of their political judgment and experience.

- **Operations Committee** — to plan and co-ordinate the operational elements of the campaign — meets weekly — members are all of the heads of the operational groups: tour, youth, communications, materials, office manager, computer operations, policy development and volunteers.

In 1985 the concept of the war room had yet to be introduced to politics. If I were writing that same report in 2016, I would add that a war room meeting should take place early each day, at 7:00 or 7:30 a.m. The campaign manager, the communications director, and the other war room specialists should attend each meeting in person or by telephone.

I would also add a short early-morning daily meeting of the operations committee to review each day's activities.

The Getty campaign came together very well, and he won the leadership.

However, my involvement came to an abrupt end shortly after my report was written. Loose lips, possibly from within the Getty organization, boasted that the campaign had recruited my services. That made my participation problematic for Don Getty. At that time, many Albertans had unfavourable attitudes about easterners, and, as one political cartoon in the *Calgary Herald* said, "How could Don Getty be so arrogant to use the talents of an easterner?"

The attitudes of Albertans to easterners appears to have moderated in the years since; I was pleased to see Brian Topp, a friend of mine and another ex-Montrealer, serve as the head of the war room for Rachel Notley in her successful campaign to become premier of Alberta in 2015.

As I said at the outset of this chapter, organization can be the difference when contests are close. Each of the following examples reinforces the need for a prospective candidate and the campaign manager to do the hard work up front of identifying and recruiting the right team personnel.

1988 FEDERAL ELECTION, ROSEDALE

I was the campaign manager for David MacDonald, a Red Tory, in Rosedale (now called University-Rosedale) during the 1988 federal election — the free trade election. A United Church clergyman, David was attempting a comeback to the House of Commons after having lost his seat in Prince Edward Island in the 1980 federal election.

His main opponent in 1988 was Liberal Bill Graham, and we knew that we were in a very close fight. Both campaigns did a good job of identifying their voters, and each campaign put aggressive plans in place to ensure that their supporters got to the polls.

I especially remember the details of our plan to get out our ethnic voters, who were a significant voting bloc in the riding. Many of these Filipino, South Asian, and Chinese voters were more comfortable communicating in their own languages, and our organizers made plans to take large groups of them to the polls with the instruction that they were to vote for number five. (MacDonald's name was the fifth on the ballot.) The Liberal team instructed their voters to vote for number four. (Graham's name was fourth.)

The final results gave number five an eighty-vote lead over number four, and David MacDonald went back to the House of Commons. The winning margin for MacDonald was barely one-third of one vote per polling station. This close election was decided by MacDonald's organization.

1992 ALBERTA PC PARTY LEADERSHIP

In 1992 I ran Elaine McCoy's campaign for the leadership of the Progressive Conservative Party of Alberta. As minister of labour in the

Don Getty government, Elaine brought many solid policy ideas to the leadership contest, but she finished second to last on the first ballot.

Elaine was not the only woman to run in that contest. Nancy Betkowski, the minister of health, finished in first place after the first ballot on November 28, 1992; out of more than 32,000 votes cast in the party-wide vote, she found herself precisely one vote — one! — ahead of Ralph Klein: 16,393 to 16,392. A second ballot was to be held a week later.

The male caucus supporters of Klein's candidacy sprang into action. Unlike the rules for many other parties, the Alberta PC contest permitted the selling of new memberships between the first and second ballots. During the next week, more than 25,000 new memberships were sold.

On December 5, 1992, organization triumphed. Ralph Klein won the leadership over Nancy Betkowski by 46,245 to 31,722, thus becoming the twelfth premier of Alberta. Meanwhile, my candidate, McCoy, received a consolation prize of sorts as many of the policies from her campaign were adopted by the Klein government over the next four years.

1995 NEWFOUNDLAND AND LABRADOR PC PARTY LEADERSHIP

I was asked by Lynn Verge to manage her campaign for leader of the Progressive Conservative Party of Newfoundland and Labrador in 1996. Lynn had worked with me on the leadership campaigns of the two previous leaders of that party, Brian Peckford and Tom Rideout. When the job became vacant, she decided to throw her hat in the ring.

She and I knew that she would be in a tough fight, because many in 1996 still did not believe a woman could be elected as a party leader. She was opposed by a fellow House of Assembly member, Loyola Sullivan. Many of the male Progressive Conservative MHAs (Members of the House of Assembly) threw their support behind Sullivan.

On the day of the convention, each candidate was given thirty minutes to make a final pitch to the delegates. Sullivan's organizers decided to place all of his male MHA supporters on the stage behind him as he made his presentation. In what was widely perceived to be tokenism, they arranged

"Landslide Lynn." In 1995, my client Lynn Verge won the PC leadership of Newfoundland and Labrador by a margin of just three votes, making her the first woman to lead a party in the province's history. Unfortunately, she could not replicate her landslide in the provincial election in early 1996. The Liberals under Brian Tobin won handily and Verge lost her own seat in the House of Assembly.

Lynn VERGE *on the Future...*

"It'll no longer be politics as usual in this province... The PCs offer sound decision-making based on an open approach, honest consultation, and legitimate team work.

It won't be like the one-man leadership of the past. The PCs have a plan for the future...the right plan, the right agenda... for the people."

VOTE FOR TRUST

NEWFOUNDLAND PC & LABRADOR

for a female high-school student to formally place Sullivan's name into nomination. The gender optics on the stage that afternoon were terrible.

I was standing in the middle of the convention floor watching this scene unfold. Three female delegates holding Sullivan signs were just in front of me. They looked at each other, and one said, "There will be no place in his party for me." They dropped their signs onto the floor.

Lynn Verge won the leadership on the first and only ballot by — you guessed it — three votes.

This close race was lost by the Sullivan organization.

Organizations that are created for most businesses or other sectors in society are built to last. Political organizations disappear just when they are operating at the top of their game. All that remains are memories and the relationships that have been developed through the course of the campaign.

Once the candidate has been selected and the organization prepared for battle, they will need certain weapons or tools with which to wage the combat that lies ahead. First and foremost will be research, the subject of the next chapter.

Chapter 6

Research Can Map the Route to Victory

He who asks is a fool for five minutes. He who does not is a fool forever.

— CHINESE PROVERB

Planning any journey, whether it is done by automobile, train, or air, requires some research and a map detailing how to arrive at your desired destination.

A political campaign is also a journey — one that has a starting point and a finish line. You cannot run a successful campaign without a map. In the case of a political campaign, that map is created with the assistance of public opinion research. You need to know what the voters are thinking. What are the important issues for them? What do they think of your candidate? What do they like — and, more important, dislike — about the candidate? Is he or she credible in their eyes? Do they believe him or her? What do they see as the candidate's strengths and weaknesses? Do voters see any character issues, potential minefields that the campaign team needs to be aware of? This information allows a campaign manager to plot a strategy or a map with a route to improve the chances for victory at the finish line.

There are essentially two kinds of research; both are important in preparing for a campaign. One is what we call "quantitative research." A sufficiently large number of respondents are interviewed so that the accuracy of the results can be quantified. The statistical "universe" that the respondents represent may be a nation, a province, or a single electoral unit. A large sample — it can number in the hundreds or thousands — is contacted by phone, Internet, or direct mail. Respondents are questioned about issues, perceptions of candidates, and their voting intentions. The accuracy of the results depends upon the number of respondents interviewed. According to the laws of probability, a sample of one hundred yields results that are accurate within plus or minus 10 percent, nineteen times out of twenty. A sample of one thousand yields results that are accurate within plus or minus 3.1 percent, nineteen times out of twenty. (What is the twentieth time? It is a rogue poll that defies the statistical probabilities with results that fall outside the anticipated margin of error. All campaign managers have encountered rogue polls. In my experience they are often produced for media outlets near the end of a campaign and are the result of shoddy methodology — that is, poor sampling, outdated field work, and/or biased questions.)

The size of the sample is often a function of available budget combined with the level of accuracy required. From these results, the campaign manager can assemble a portrait of the electorate that the manager and the candidate will be working to convince to support.

The second kind is "qualitative research." Twelve randomly selected groups of voters are assembled to discuss the issues. These focus groups work this way: a relatively small number of voters, maybe eight or twelve, selected to represent a particular universe of electors, is brought together in one focus group facility, or a boardroom or hotel room, where they are questioned in depth about issues, attributes of candidates, campaign tactics, the effectiveness of media ads, and so on — anything the campaign manager needs to know to create or fine-tune the election strategy.

Focus group research can be used effectively as exploratory research, before or in the early stages of a campaign, to identify and catalogue the range of attitudes and opinions regarding issues and personalities in the universe. This intelligence can then be used in developing a follow-up quantitative strategic survey to collect statistically reliable data on the attitudes and beliefs of the general voting population and various target groups. The insights from the groups help to ensure that nothing important is being overlooked.

Focus groups can also be used for in-depth analysis of specific issues or personality evaluations. The perceptions gleaned from these discussions with voters provide a depth of understanding that is difficult to get from quantitative research alone. This kind of research allows you to ferret out not only what attitudes and opinions voters have, but also what key factors are influencing or shaping those attitudes. Armed with this information, one is well on the way to developing an effective campaign strategy.

Focus groups in a boardroom or a hotel room are done with a TV camera placed in the room used by the respondents and the moderator. Observers watch the proceedings on a monitor in an adjoining room. In a focus group facility, a one-way mirror allows observers to watch and hear the respondents in much the same fashion as a police lineup on a television crime show. The results of the findings from such a small group of individuals cannot be said to be accurate within a range of percentage points. However, because the participants are randomly selected, the results will offer a clear indication of how the universe that is being surveyed generally feels about a range of issues.

Usually the groups are watched by various officials in the campaign — the communications director, policy chair, organization director, and senior advisers. Only a campaign manager very certain of his candidate's ability to absorb cruel personal comments will invite the candidate to observe the proceedings or to watch the videotapes later.

In summary, quantitative research tells you what people think, and qualitative research tells you why.

When I started as national director of the PC Party of Canada in 1973, MOR (Market Opinion Research) of Detroit was the party's supplier of market research services. Bob Teeter, a Republican, was a principal in that firm. Teeter also provided the same services to the Ontario PC Party and Bill Davis for much of the 1970s.

In 1976 Bill Neville was the head of opposition research for Joe Clark, the newly elected leader of the federal party. Bill felt that as one of the major federal parties the PC Party should have a Canadian pollster. As a first step, he decided to establish an in-house research unit using his staff resources and purchasing computer time from Carleton University to do the data processing. He canvassed members of his staff and three volunteers applied: Allan Gregg, Stephen Probyn, and Ian Green.

That was when I first met Allan Gregg. I got to work with him directly on a number of federal and provincial by-elections and studies for some of our provincial parties.

By 1979, the Ontario PC Party was also looking for a Canadian pollster. Allan Gregg went into the private sector and formed Decima Research, which became one of Canada's pre-eminent research firms in the 1980s and 1990s. Gregg became the pollster for Bill Davis.

I have worked with Allan on a number of occasions, federally and provincially, in the years since. He is the best researcher I have ever come across. He is able to look at a large volume of data or listen to a number of focus groups and put together a succinct story of what the findings suggest to a particular candidate or party leader.

In the early days at Decima, Gregg undertook a project to determine which factors drove success in local riding elections. He assembled and analyzed all of the Ontario polling results from the 1975 and 1977 Ontario provincial elections.

Allan reported that the number-one factor in predicting success was name recognition: the candidate with the highest level of name recognition was much more likely to win. As he described the research findings to me shortly after, he said dryly. "If people don't know your name when they enter the voting station, you are unlikely to win."

While that is usually the case, there have been elections where the opposite occurs. One was the surprise election of Bob Rae and the NDP in Ontario in 1990; on election day voters were observed asking election officials for the names of the NDP candidates in the polling stations. Another was the large number of MPs elected in Quebec by Jack Layton and the NDP in 2011, one of whom spent much of her campaign in Las Vegas. However, in the majority of elections candidates will simply not win if they have not made themselves known to the voters.

Allan then reported that the second most important factor in predicting success was the level of favourability of the candidate. "If two candidates have the same level of name recognition, then the candidate with the highest favourability rating will probably win."

I have seen these factors play out many times over the last forty-five years.

The most recent example was the 2015 federal election where Justin Trudeau had the highest favourability rating and Stephen Harper had the lowest. In the week before the election Harper's net favourability rating was *minus* 24 percent. That meant that 24 percent more voters had an unfavourable impression of Harper than had a favourable impression. It is almost impossible to get elected with those numbers!

In the bookmark prepared as a sales tool for my book with Geoffrey Stevens, *Leaders and Lesser Mortals,* I provided advice demonstrating the importance that I attach to research: "Poll even when broke."

My rule of thumb is that between 10 and 15 percent of the overall campaign budget should be allocated for research. You may be able to get away with less if news organizations are actively polling and publishing the results. The problem is, much media polling these days is provided free of charge by polling organizations looking for free publicity. They use media polls as loss leaders for their commercial business. A polling company can attract clients by telling them it does polling for CBC or the *Globe and Mail*, but be wary. Something that is free usually does not give a campaign manager the quality or the type of information that the manager and the candidate really require.

Let's step back for a moment and review the various uses for research in a political campaign. These uses range broadly:

- From simply helping to understand the results and the reasons behind the results of the ballot question to obtaining information and insights that will form the basis for the overall campaign strategy
- From testing reactions to communications materials to understanding the public's thinking on major policy issues in depth
- From understanding the strengths and weaknesses of your candidate and his or her opponents to designing the question for a national referendum
- From determining when a leader should call an election to recognizing when he or she should step down and retire

While the above are all good uses of research, I often see newspaper headlines that predict the future based upon quantitative polling. This is not a reliable use of research. Quite simply, a poll is a snapshot at one point in time; it is not a predictor of the future.

Misuse of polling leads to erroneous predictions — such as "Bob Rae will never be elected premier of Ontario" (which he was in 1990) or "Rachel Notley and the NDP can never win Alberta" (which they did in 2015). I came to the conclusion long ago that the word "never" should never be used in politics. Politics is the most unpredictable of professions. Anything can happen — and probably will.

While newspapers often get it wrong in reading the polls, from time to time pollsters themselves also seem to fall into the same trap. In 2013, Darrell Bricker, pollster and CEO of Ipsos Public Affairs Worldwide, and John Ibbitson, the *Globe and Mail*'s chief political correspondent, co-authored a book, *The Big Shift*. It was mainly based on the results of a large exit poll conducted on the evening of the 2011 federal election, coupled with an analysis of the demographic changes brought about by recent immigration in Ontario — immigration that supposedly produced a population much more in favour of lower taxes, more criminals in prison, less bureaucracy, and an iron grip on the public purse strings. Also added to the mix was the effect of the resource-driven economic gains in western Canada. The authors predicted that these changes *"will make Canada inexorably a more conservative place* [emphasis added]," with progressives and liberals on the wrong side of demography.

And then along came Justin Trudeau in 2015 to give the big shaft to the big shift. He proved once again that polls, especially those conducted years earlier, cannot be used to predict the future.

I can best illustrate the good uses of research by describing examples from a few campaigns, some of which I worked on and some where I was simply an interested observer.

1980 FEDERAL ELECTION

Doug Hurley, an associate of mine from Goldfarb Consultants, recalls an instance when focus groups were not only used to assess which ads in a campaign were working best, but also how the team could increase the ads' effectiveness.

> You may remember the 1980 campaign versus Joe Clark featured a very effective Liberal commercial that was called "The Magician." The ad featured a magician's house of cards, representing Joe Clark's election platform, with each individual card representing a plank in that plat- form. Research had identified which of those policy platforms were weak or unpopular with soft Liberals, undecided and swing voters — the big one being Clark's proposed eighteen cents per gallon gasoline tax. In the ad, the magician pulled a weak or unpopular policy card out of the house of cards — one at a time — until the house collapsed. The ad worked because it made voters very uneasy with Clark's platform. It helped to galvanize opposition to the Clark government by drawing on the strong opposition that already existed to the proposed gas tax.
>
> But in focus group pre-testing of the first version of the "Magician" ad we found that the house of cards collapsed prematurely, diminishing its effectiveness. Not enough "unpopular" policy cards were pulled out before the collapse. The research indicated that pulling out at least one more "unpopular" policy card would greatly improve the ad's impact and effectiveness.
>
> The value of this kind of focus group research was clearly understood by our campaign director, Senator (Keith) Davey. After presenting these findings to him, he said: "I knew there was something wrong with that ad, but I just didn't know what it was. And that's it!"

The ad was revised to add an additional card pull and it worked extremely well.

1983 PC PARTY OF CANADA LEADERSHIP CONVENTION

There are many reasons for politicians to use public opinion research, but one of them should not be to decide whether to become a candidate. This one decision belongs solely to a candidate and should not be made by advisers or pollsters. If a candidate needs to be convinced to run by polling numbers, he or she is in the wrong game.

Early in my career as a campaign manager, I watched John Crosbie demonstrate the importance of candidate conviction, even in the face of bad polling numbers. Immediately following the 1983 Progressive Conservative national meeting in Winnipeg, where Joe Clark, disappointed with his support, had called on the party to hold a leadership convention, I asked Allan Gregg to conduct a poll among delegates likely to attend the convention a few months later. The results were bleak. They were bleaker than bleak! The poll showed that Crosbie could expect the support of no more than 3 percent of the delegates. That was far less than prospective candidates Peter Lougheed (premier of Alberta), Bill Davis (premier of Ontario), Joe Clark (the incumbent), and Brian Mulroney (the eventual winner). Yet Crosbie was totally unfazed by the results, and we set about to plan his campaign using many of the insights gained from that research.

Years later I read with interest his recollection of those numbers in his memoir, *No Holds Barred,* published in 1997. He wrote:

> My primary reason for running was this: I thought I was the best person to lead the party and to win the next general election. If you think you are the best man or woman available for a position, you should go after it, no matter how heavy the odds may seem to be against you. And if you don't think you are the best person — if you don't think you're the greatest — you shouldn't be in the game.

Going up the middle strategy works — sometimes. A *Toronto Sun* cartoon published in the last week of the 1983 PC leadership campaign. I was spinning a theory that Crosbie could go up the middle between Clark and Mulroney. He couldn't!

Crosbie did not win that leadership contest in June 1983, but he put on a strong campaign, coming within two hundred votes of Clark and Mulroney before he was eliminated at the end of the third ballot. Nobody called him a loser for long. When the new leader, Mulroney, became prime minister in 1984, he used Crosbie in a number of key roles, none more important than introducing free trade with the United States. It was a policy that Crosbie had vigorously advocated — and Mulroney had opposed — during the leadership race.

1984 FEDERAL ELECTION

Immediately following Mulroney's victory in the 1983 leadership race, he asked me to go to Ottawa to work with Norman Atkins and put together the campaign organization for the federal election expected to be called

"For Lash – who has done so much for the party – With gratitude, Brian." I spent eight months in Ottawa putting together the organization for the 1984 election.

in 1984. Norman was the campaign chair and I was the director of organization. I spent the following seven months in Ottawa putting the campaign structure together.

It took us some time before we were able to decide which pollster we would use. Norman and I found it difficult to put together a plan in the absence of research, but Mulroney wanted to be sure of the choice of pollster. Allan Gregg had worked with Norman and me before, and he was our choice. Mulroney was slow to agree, though.

I understood Mulroney's hesitation in making a decision, as the relationship between a leader and a pollster is very close, and Mulroney did not know Gregg. The subject of pollster selection came up frequently during our weekly meetings with Mulroney to review campaign planning. However, it would be February 1984 before a decision was finally made.

Atkins was away on vacation in Aruba, and instead of our weekly meeting, Mulroney phoned me at headquarters. He had obviously been thinking of research, and he raised the issue. He said he was hesitant to make a decision because he had never seen Gregg's work; perhaps we should commission him to do a poll of Toronto so that Mulroney might understand what Gregg would bring to the table.

I pushed back and said that what we desperately needed was a baseline study for the country. Mulroney immediately agreed.

The rest of the story about the relationship between Gregg and Mulroney is well known. Allan and Mulroney worked together well and successfully both in 1984 and especially in 1988, when his advice about "bombing the bridge of trust" that John Turner, the Liberal leader, had established with Canadian voters turned the "free trade election" around in our favour.

All candidates should consider their choice of pollster carefully. They will usually be spending time together in pressure situations, and they need to be able to work together well.

The numbers never lie. Brian Mulroney, John Tory, and 1988 PC campaign chair and pollster Allan Gregg at Harrington Lake after a briefing session.

1986 B.C. SOCIAL CREDIT LEADERSHIP CONVENTION

Stuart Douglas Boland Smith, to give him his full name, was the chief of staff for the Social Credit premier of British Columbia, Bill Bennett. When Bennett resigned in 1986, "Bud" Smith decided to seek the Social Credit leadership.

Smith hired me to help run his campaign. I immediately began organizing things so that the necessary research could be conducted. I had used research in most of my campaigns, having initially gone with Decima Research, Environics, Canadian Facts, and a few smaller research firms. In Bud Smith's campaign I hooked up with Martin Goldfarb, who had been prominent in federal politics as the Liberal Party pollster for Pierre Trudeau. Marty knew Bud Smith from the days when he had done polling for Bill Bennett. He liked Smith and offered to help with his leadership campaign. We arranged for Goldfarb to research Smith's support among delegates to the leadership convention, to be held a few weeks later in Whistler, B.C.

We got the numbers a couple of weeks before the convention, and they were worse than we had feared. They forecast that Bud would finish no better than third, far behind Bill Vander Zalm, whom the poll showed winning in a landslide over eleven other candidates. Many candidates would have been crushed by this news, but Smith took the results in stride. In retrospect, I understood the value of the poll. It gave my candidate two weeks, and not just twenty minutes, to think about his future and to decide what he would do when the first-ballot results were announced. When they were, Bud walked immediately across the floor to Vander Zalm and threw his support to him. Appreciative of the gesture, the new leader made Smith his attorney general when he was sworn in as premier. Bud was elected MLA for Kamloops in the subsequent provincial election.

When I returned to Toronto, Martin Goldfarb persuaded me to join his survey firm, Goldfarb Consultants, arguing that if I learned the research business I would be able to do my own polling for my political campaigns. He also made the not insignificant point that between elections I would be able to make a living doing research for non-political clients. Good advice. That is how I have kept bread on the table ever since.

WINDSOR, ONTARIO, 1992

I vividly recall an experience in 1992 with a newly elected mayor of Windsor, Ontario, Mike Hurst. Mike was interested in understanding what role research could play for him in his new role as mayor. I suggested that interviews with some focus groups could be of value in understanding how people were reacting to the first few months of his term. I arranged for Mike to watch the interviews with these groups from an adjoining hotel room, as there were no focus group facilities in Windsor.

Near the conclusion of the interview with the first of the two groups that night, I went to the observer room to ask Mike and other observers whether there were any other questions that I should ask the respondents. He started by saying, "Lasch, where did you get these people? They can't possibly live in Windsor. They don't know what a great job I am doing!" I assured him that indeed these people had been recruited from his city — and that perhaps they were not to blame if they did not know what he had been doing. Perhaps it was poor communications on his part or his office's. Mike quickly learned how to get his message out. He went on to be re-elected for three more terms as mayor.

1997 UNITED KINGDOM GENERAL ELECTION

In 1996, I had an opportunity to conduct research in the United Kingdom in advance of the general election that was held in early May 1997.

Prime Minister John Major, the leader of Britain's Conservative party who had succeeded the "Iron Lady," Margaret Thatcher, had been trailing badly in the polls for quite some time during his third term. Goldfarb Consultants did a substantial amount of automotive research for Ford Motor Company both in North America and abroad. Martin Goldfarb was contacted by the then chairman of Ford U.K., who was a big supporter of John Major and who, like many in the business community, was concerned that Tony Blair and his Labour Party were going to sweep into office.

Martin proposed that we conduct a series of focus groups in the U.K. and provide a second opinion to Prime Minister Major and his campaign director, Sir Brian Mawhinney.

I was sent to London and conducted ten focus groups over a six-day period in three cities — London, Bolton (in the north), and Bristol (in the southwest). I returned to Toronto and prepared my report; one week later I returned to present our findings with Marty Goldfarb. The key finding of this research was that the slogan being used by the Conservative Party was misguided and was actually helping Tony Blair and Labour. The slogan — "New Labour, New Danger" — reassured many who had feared the old Labour Party as free-spending socialists but were prepared to look at them with fresh eyes if they were "new."

John Major and his party had been scarred by a number of sex and other scandals, and by party disunity over entry to the European Union, and were facing a strong desire for change after eighteen years of Conservative government. They were trailing Labour by close to 50 percent in the public polls. John Major himself was seen as grey and boring, but was also seen as trustworthy. While the public was inclined to support Tony Blair, who came across as an exciting leader, they were also suspicious of him. A female focus group respondent in London put it succinctly. "When I see that man on the telly I know he has his fingers crossed behind his back when he is talking."

I made the point to Mawhinney that the target for the Conservatives should not be New Labour but rather Tony Blair. I put my middle finger to my forehead and said, "You have to put a bullet between his eyes. He is the target you need to destroy, not New Labour." As I stood there, I suspected he did not really understand my insights and probably thought I was just a crazy person from the colonies.

The strategists seemed to reject my advice, and the Conservatives were still trailing by 50 percent when the short, three-week election campaign began in April 1997. In the middle of the campaign, however, they switched tactics and started to attack Blair as being untrustworthy. The gap shrank considerably, and on election night, May 1, 1997, the Labour lead had shrunk to 12 percent over the Conservatives. But it was too little, too late. The Conservatives had their worst showing since 1906. With the assistance of Bill Clinton's political team from Washington, which showed Labour how to set up and operate a campaign war room, Tony Blair became the new prime minister.

2000 FEDERAL ELECTION

Joe Clark left public life in 1993, the year when Brian Mulroney, in whose Cabinet he had served, retired and was succeeded by Kim Campbell. The ensuing general election was a disaster for the Tories. The Liberals, under the leadership of Jean Chrétien, won a majority government, and the mighty PCs were reduced to a rump of two seats, one in Quebec and one in New Brunswick. A new PC leader, Jean Charest, succeeded in pulling the PCs back from the brink, winning twenty seats in the 1997 election. The following year, however, Charest switched arenas and parties. He moved to provincial politics and took over the leadership of the Quebec Liberal Party. Five years later he was premier of Quebec, a position he would hold for nine years.

When Charest left for Quebec, Clark returned and in 1999 recaptured the party leadership he had lost to Mulroney more than a decade earlier. He was anxious to secure a seat in the House of Commons before the Liberals called another general election. Scott Brison, the Progressive Conservative MP for Kings-Hants in Nova Scotia (and today a sitting Liberal MP and president of the Treasury Board in Justin Trudeau's government) gave up his seat so Clark could run in a by-election, which was held in September 2000.

I had received a number of telephone calls from Conservative Senator Con Di Nino, who entreated me to consider running the party's next federal campaign. I put off making a decision but eventually agreed to meet Clark in late August to have a discussion. Clark was campaigning in Kings-Hants for the upcoming by-election, and I was on my way to Newfoundland to go salmon fishing.

We agreed to meet in his future riding during a layover on my flight to St. John's. Early in our conversation I told Clark that part of my hesitancy in accepting the position as campaign manager was that a number of people had told me that he did not accept advice. To his credit, he looked me straight in the eye and said that he did not take "bad "advice.

I could not argue with that, so I called him after spending time on the river in Newfoundland and accepted his offer.

Clark won the Kings-Hants by-election held on September 11, 2000, and I was introduced to the Tory caucus as the national campaign manager the following morning. I now had a new assignment, one with great possibilities — and even greater challenges. The party was $5 million in debt and we needed to count on the benevolence of our bankers to allow us to run a campaign. Charest's departure had been a body blow to the party. We were mired in fourth place in the polls, at 6 percent, or lower, depending on the survey. We had a handful of nominated candidates. Not least, with the general election expected before the end of the fall, we knew we had barely three or four weeks to prepare. My first priority, after meeting with the caucus, was to commission some research, and then to arrange a meeting with the banks and the national executive of the party to come to an understanding as to how much each would let me spend.

In fact, the banks were great! Their attitudes seemed to be in for a penny, in for a pound. We would be allowed to spend up to $5 million for the campaign. The national executive of the Party was just as supportive.

The research was equally successful. I decided that a number of focus groups would give us the insights needed to run a campaign. There was little point in spending a lot of money for a large quantitative poll that would show us at 5 or 6 percent. I already knew that. The challenge was to understand how we could take votes away from the Liberal Party and/ or the right-wing Canadian Alliance, both of whom were polling significantly ahead of us. If we could not attract votes from one or the other of these parties, we would be stranded at 6 percent — in which case we would not win twelve seats, the minimum required for official party status in the House of Commons.

We conducted ten focus groups — two each in Toronto, Montreal, Vancouver, Calgary, and Halifax. There was no point in talking to individuals who were fixed in their voting intentions. We recruited one group of soft Liberals and one group of soft Canadian Alliance voters in each city. (By soft supporters I mean individuals who said they would vote

Liberal or Canadian Alliance that day but were open to changing their minds before the election.)

I could have saved half of the research money if we had talked only to soft Liberals. The "soft" Canadian Alliance supporters were beyond our reach. They were extremely angry at our party. They had come to the Alliance from the populist, right-wing protest movement, the Reform Party. If they left the Alliance they would vote for the New Democrats before they would consider the Tories. It was the first time I had seen such a huge attitudinal swing from right to left. I came to understand that this was a vote against the establishment and big government. I got to see the phenomenon again in two mayoral races in Toronto a decade and more later.

The results from the soft Liberal voters were much more encouraging. They feared the Canadian Alliance, and if they left the Liberal Party they would vote Progressive Conservative. I then had to find out why they were soft supporters of the Liberal Party and see what we could do to motivate them to switch to us.

The conversation in the groups generally went like this:

Q: Why are you a soft Liberal?
A: Jean Chrétien.
Q: What is it about Jean Chrétien that you don't like?
A: He is a liar.
Q: What did he lie about?
A: The GST. The Free Trade Agreement. And a number of other smaller promises.

That was it. We had to go after soft Liberals with the message that Jean Chrétien was a liar.

That would be easier said than done.

In 1993 the Conservatives under Kim Campbell had been decimated, reduced to just two seats. During the election her campaign had attacked Chrétien with an ad that featured Chrétien's partially paralyzed face. The public outcry was so great that the Tories had to withdraw the ad and Campbell had to apologize to Chrétien. Now I was going to have to find a safe way to call the same Liberal leader a liar. I was certain of one thing. The ads would not use Chrétien's photo.

I presented the results of the research to John Bowen and Eric Bell from our ad agency in Toronto, Bowen and Binstock, who came up with two very humorous television spots that called Chrétien a liar in an acceptable manner.

The first ad was a take-off on the K-Tel television ads of the 1960s. These were hard-sell ads designed to market music records — "Twenty original hits! Twenty original stars! Phone and get your copy today!"

The Chrétien ad started with, "Get your copy of Jean Chrétien's 101 Greatest Lies! Hear the whopper about cancelling the GST."

The second ad showed a picture of the Liberal Party Red Book, containing Chrétien's promises from his first campaign in 1993. By 2000 a large number of those promises had not been kept, although Chrétien had once proclaimed that hell would freeze over before he broke any of the promises. The ad showed the Red Book on a table being buffeted by strong winds. The pages started to blow open. Then the rain began, and a loud god-like voice boomed out the Chrétien quote about hell freezing over. The book was struck by a bolt of lightning and started to burn.

I talked by phone with Clark about the research and the scripts for the two ads. His reaction was a deep belly laugh. He never saw the ads before we ran them on the eve of the first televised leaders' debate in Ottawa. He was true to his word in Kings-Hants. He never did listen to bad advice — only to good advice. He allowed me to manage the campaign and to produce the ads that were designed by the research.

On election night, November 27, 2000, the PCs won twelve seats, just enough to retain official party status. We had managed to carve out an additional 6 percent of the electorate, mainly from soft Liberals. Clark himself won the twelfth seat in Calgary Centre by defeating popular Canadian Alliance MP Eric Lowther. (Early in the campaign I had commissioned a poll in Calgary Centre to see how bad it was. It was worse than bad! Clark was polling at 7 percent of the vote against Lowther, whose support was over 50 percent. I told Joe that I had done the poll. He never asked about the result and I never told him. I knew that he knew how tough the challenge was; I didn't have to tell him.)

Nothing like a hanging in the morning to focus your attention. Joe Clark and me on the occasion of the unveiling of his portrait in the House of Commons, Ottawa, 2008.

Clark defeated Lowther by 46 percent to 39 percent. His decision to run in Calgary, in the heart of the Alliance stronghold, was an act of political courage, and I believe this demonstration of courage was a major factor in Joe's victory that night. This was an example of voters making a decision on their perceptions of the human values of a candidate as opposed to perceptions of winnability or policies.

2007 ONTARIO PROVINCIAL ELECTION

John Tory was elected leader of the Ontario Progressive Conservative party in September 2004. For Tory, a lawyer, business executive, and long-time political backroom operative, this was his second entry into elective politics. He had run for mayor of Toronto the previous year, losing to David Miller in a close contest. Despite the fact that I had managed Miller's campaign, Tory asked me to manage both his leadership campaign and then the provincial campaign in 2007.

By late 2006 we had decided that the party should spend some money before the writ on TV ads intended to define Tory to the electorate before our opponents did the job for us. Three thirty-second spots were created: one general ad on Tory's personal background as a businessman and community volunteer, and one each on the two most important issues at the time, the economy and health care.

We decided to convene focus groups for a "disaster check" on the ads, despite the fact that the campaign team felt very positive about them. The background and economy ads each passed the check.

Health care was ranked the number one issue in the province at that time. A great deal of political rhetoric was being expended on making the system more efficient by authorizing nurses to perform certain tasks traditionally done by more highly paid doctors. The ad we put together showed John Tory discussing this approach with a group of nursing students. He told them, "You have to do more and different things in your role as nurses in our health-care system." We thought that it showed Tory being knowledgeable about future changes required in the health field. However, the focus group participants thought Tory was blaming the nurses for the problems rather than challenging them to participate in a revised role in the system.

The health-care ad went into the trash can and was never aired. (For other reasons I will discuss in Chapter 12, where I write about party discipline, John Tory's whole campaign was dumped into the trash can by Ontario voters in the 2007 election.)

This illustrates one of the great values of using focus groups to test all campaign communications materials. People can often pick up on a single word, phrase, or image in a piece of communication that can create or convey the wrong message, or confuse and undercut the effectiveness of the communication. And unless the problem is caught and fixed, you multiply the mistake every time you air the material.

"Never wise to count chickens . . . " Cartoon showing John Tory as leader of the Opposition in Ontario contemplating how he would deal with Toronto mayor David Miller in the future. The cartoon is signed by David Miller: "Lasch, Only in his dreams! — David."

2014 TORONTO MAYORAL ELECTION

The findings of the research for Olivia Chow in early 2014 created a dilemma for the mayoralty candidate and her campaign team. After three years with Rob Ford as mayor, two-thirds of Torontonians were ready for a change — ready for a new mayor.

We had organized both qualitative and quantitative studies. Our research showed voters placed high importance on the next mayor being much more progressive than Ford, and less embarrassing. They wanted a mayor who would invest in community programs and supports for the residents who needed them most, a mayor who would maintain city services (as opposed to cutting taxes), and a mayor who would dedicate himself or herself to making Toronto neighbourhoods more livable for families. This much was welcome news for Olivia. However, it was not all good news. One-half of the voters also thought that Rob Ford's "Stop the Gravy Train" agenda had been good for Toronto, and they placed high importance on the next mayor being someone who would keep city spending under control.

In short, the citizens of Toronto wanted a pragmatic progressive — or perhaps a fiscal conservative reformer — to be their next mayor.

These findings put Olivia Chow in a tight spot. As a member of the NDP, she automatically received the benefit of being seen as progressive, but at the same time she was not seen as someone who would control city spending — rather quite the opposite. In fact, some focus group respondents labelled her a "tax-and-spend socialist."

We had many tense discussions. How should we position Olivia? Should we accentuate her positives or try to minimize her weaknesses? We decided to adopt a defensive posture. We would present her story: as a child growing up in a poor immigrant family that needed to watch every penny it spent, and as an adult politician who had produced seven consecutive balanced budgets as a member of conservative Mayor Mel Lastman's budget committee.

We realized that by spending our available time and effort building a line of defence against fiscal irresponsibility, we would have less opportunity to promote Olivia's progressive values. For better or worse, we chose to build the defence. (A look at another side of our campaign strategy is found in Chapter 2, and Chapter 8 looks at the people we chose to put it before the voters.)

The initial phase of the campaign went well. Our voter support held up. But in the middle of the summer of 2014 our progressive base in the downtown wards started sending us a message. They were leaving Olivia to support John Tory. They felt that he was a real conservative who would control spending, and at the same time he was progressive enough, at least compared to Rob Ford, to satisfy their desire for a progressive mayor.

Political scientists will debate our decision for years to come. Did we err in our decision to shore up Olivia's fiscal credentials at the expense of her progressive values? Or was she doomed from the start by the political cards she was dealt?

2015 ALBERTA PROVINCIAL ELECTION

Jim Prentice, former federal Cabinet minister in the Harper government, was elected leader of the Progressive Conservative Party of Alberta in September 2014. In the normal course of events the next provincial election would have been held in 2016. Extensive polling indicated there was no great public desire for an early election and no indication of an obvious winner.

Nevertheless, Prentice called an early election in May 2015. His party was soundly defeated by Rachel Notley and the NDP.

Jim Prentice learned, as David Peterson had in 1990, that calling an early election is risky. The public expects consistency; anything short of a convincing reason for the unexpected will not persuade the voters to support you.

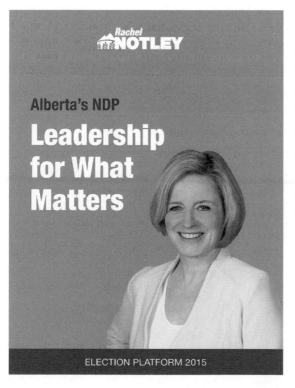

The word "never" should never be used in politics. Rachel Notley, in a big surprise, became the new NDP premier of Alberta in 2015. My friend Brian Topp, an ex-Montrealer, ran her war room during the election and currently serves as her chief of staff.

2015 FEDERAL ELECTION

Nightly tracking with quantitative rolling polls has long been used to track the movement and progress of campaigns. Looking at the entrails of a campaign on a nightly basis, though, can be very discouraging for a campaign manager. The nightly results are usually kept within a small group of people in the campaign. On some occasions even the candidate is not given the results. On a morning when the overnights were positive, it is easy to go into headquarters with a smile. On other days it is tough, but the same smile has to be there.

This nightly tracking is especially important during the last few weeks of a campaign and can provide insights that can reinforce or alter current messaging. I have found through my use of nightly tracking that there can be significant movement in voter intention right up to the last evening, and even on voting day. It is therefore important to continue this tracking until the last evening.

For the first time in a federal or provincial election in Canada, Nanos Research was commissioned by the *Globe and Mail* and CTV to conduct nightly tracking for the 2015 election, and these results were published online each morning. No longer would campaign managers be forced to paste on fake smiles when they went to work. Everybody in their world knew what was happening.

The Nanos Research predictions of voter intentions mirrored the actual results on election day. (Chapters 1, 2, and 7 look at some of the reasons for the Liberal campaign's success.) The tracking accurately detected a 3 to 4 percent drop in NDP support on the final weekend and an almost equal corresponding increase in Liberal support. The need to continue tracking right up until the end was validated by how close the final Nanos figures came to the outcome on election night.

While it is discouraging when your advice is ignored and gratifying when it is accepted, the point I am making is that research is just one tool in the toolbox of a political campaign, and the advice gleaned from the research is just that: advice. In the end leaders have the right and the responsibility to make the final call on how their campaign is operated. After all, it is their name that is on the ballot, not that of their pollster or campaign manager.

However, candidates who do not utilize the benefits of research of all types are placing themselves at a competitive disadvantage. As David Ogilvy, often referred to as the "father of advertising," said, "Advertising people who ignore research are as dangerous as generals who ignore decodes of enemy signals."

If the research is done correctly, the insights provided and the candidate's core values and principles will combine to create the strategic plan that will have the best chance for success. Nineteen times out of twenty, the numbers do not lie.

An important component of the strategic plan will be the vision and policies that form part of the campaign platform. By putting the research chapter ahead of the chapter on vision and policies, I am not suggesting that the results of the research alone drive the policies that wind up in a platform. The personal values, experiences, and policy preferences of the candidate need to be meshed with the research results in order to create an effective platform. In my view the research is needed up front on a whole range of issues, including policy, and it is imperative to obtain an early benchmark on many of these before proceeding.

In the next chapter, I will deal with the role of vision and policies and, more important, I will explain how these translate into the perceptions of values that voters want in their elected officials.

Chapter 7

The Role of Vision, Policy, and Values

This is the vision. One Canada — One Canada — where Canadians will have preserved to them the control of their own economic and political destiny. Sir John A. Macdonald saw Canada from east to west. He opened the west. I see a new Canada — a Canada of the North. This is the vision.

— JOHN GEORGE DIEFENBAKER

Vision, policies, and values each play a role in the success or failure of political campaigns. The truth is, though, that relatively few campaigns are run on a big idea or vision. In fact, most campaigns are based on policies that, while serviceable, fall short of being visionary.

Yet the most memorable and effective campaigns and candidates are those that are able to tie policies together with vision. Vision should be looked on as an aspirational goal or statement that describes the difference that a candidate wants to make by his or her election. Policies are the programs or initiatives that assist the candidate in fulfilling his or her vision.

Most politicians campaign on policy platforms that they believe address the issues of the day. The issues traditionally range from the economy, health care, justice, and personal safety to foreign affairs, immigration, education, gender equality, and whatever the current policy flavour of the minute is — whether it is niqabs, electoral reform, or not allowing jets to operate out of Billy Bishop Airport on the Toronto Islands.

I can identify only a few striking examples of politicians who started with a big idea or vision — the kind that indicates where the politician sees the country, province, or city going in the years ahead.

Sir John A. Macdonald, with his vision in 1867 of One Canada from east to west, was the first politician to excite Canadians. He buttressed his vision with policies to encourage and support the construction of the trans-Canada railway.

John Diefenbaker was another. In 1958 he invited Canadians to "Join John" in embracing his vision of a Canada that included Canada's north. He won a huge majority government entirely due to support from Canadians in the south.

Ten years after Diefenbaker proclaimed his vision, Pierre Trudeau became prime minister with his vision of Canada: "the Just Society." Trudeau defined the Just Society as a nation where the rights of minorities would be safe from the whims of intolerant majorities, and where citizens would be actively involved in the development of a country that ensured equality of opportunity.

He first used the term during the 1968 Liberal Party leadership contest. It eventually came to be applied to all of his policies, from multiculturalism to criminal law reform to the *Canadian Charter of Rights and Freedoms*. There is little doubt that, regardless of what people liked or disliked about Pierre Trudeau, he was successful in pursuing policies to help fulfill his vision.

During the period from 1979 to 1985, Premier Brian Peckford of Newfoundland and Labrador campaigned on a vision to make his province a prosperous region of Canada. Newfoundland had long been a "have-not" province and annually received equalization payments from the "have" provinces. His rallying cry was "Have-not will be no more!" His policy was to push the federal government to give Newfoundland control over, and a share of, offshore mineral and oil resources and revenues. In 1985, the federal government enacted the Canada-Newfoundland Atlantic Accord which did just that. He was greatly assisted by prominent Progressive Conservative politicians of the day: Prime Minister Brian Mulroney, who signed the accord; John Crosbie, the federal political minister for Newfoundland and Labrador, who worked tirelessly for the policy; and Joe Clark, who had signalled his support during his brief tenure as prime minister in 1979.

In 1988 Canadians were once again presented with a vision, this time by Mulroney and his Conservative government. The Canada-U.S. Free Trade Agreement was a policy that demonstrated their vision that Canada should be a confident and outward-looking nation by developing closer economic ties with the United States.

John Crosbie had championed free trade with the United States during his 1983 leadership bid. Mulroney had opposed it at that time, but had later become convinced of the benefits of such a treaty. He and President Ronald Reagan signed the Free Trade Agreement (FTA) on January 2, 1988.

The Liberal-controlled Senate of Canada held up parliamentary approval of the agreement, and both the Liberals and the NDP promised to tear up the agreement if they won the next election.

Not long after the signing, on March 31, 1988, Crosbie called me with his news. He was about to be asked to take over as minister of international trade to oversee the implementation of the FTA and to sell the agreement to the Canadian public. Mulroney could see that the FTA was going to be an important issue in the election that was due within next twelve months, and he wanted Crosbie to be responsible for the file. He knew that John was passionately committed to this economic vision for Canada.

John told me he was going to say yes to Mulroney but that he wanted me to return to Ottawa and run the free trade campaign for him. He saw this assignment as being similar to a traditional political campaign and he wanted it run by someone he had previously worked with.

I went to Ottawa for five months to manage the FTA campaign. We utilized many of the tools that are part and parcel of a political campaign. We had a field organization with provincial organizers, a campaign office, a communications group that prepared speaking notes for Crosbie and other ministers and government spokespersons, and a speakers' bureau that provided individuals to speak to groups or the media about the FTA. The communications materials we produced included three million copies of a pamphlet to educate Canadians about the FTA. We also conducted extensive research among Canadians to prepare our strategic plan for the campaign, to create the effective messaging to position the FTA, and to regularly monitor its acceptance by the public.

Mulroney was later proved correct about the importance of the FTA as a political issue, as the 1988 election became known as the "free trade election."

I wish that I could say that the work done by our FTA campaign group and the three million brochures were responsible for Mulroney's re-election that fall, but the credit for that mainly belongs to Mulroney himself. His performance in the election, including his debates with John Turner, the Liberal leader, convinced enough Canadians that he, and not Turner, was telling the truth about the impact of the FTA. Notwithstanding research findings that a majority of Canadians did not support the agreement, Mulroney's (and Crosbie's) vision of a confident, outward-looking country was endorsed. On November 21, 1988, Mulroney was rewarded with a second consecutive majority government.

This turned out to be an election where people voted on their perceptions of the human values being demonstrated by the candidates (in this case, trust on the issue) and not on the specifics of the FTA, a document so complex and lengthy that even Crosbie admitted he had not read all of it.

Over the past forty-five years I have been involved with a number of campaigns where policy, without any big idea or vision, has played a featured role in deciding the final outcome. Some have been successful, while others have not. What makes the difference?

Let's look at the following examples.

1974 FEDERAL ELECTION

In 1974, as national director of the federal Progressive Conservative Party, I had a front row seat for an election in which policy played a major role. Progressive Conservative leader Robert Stanfield campaigned on a promise to introduce wage and price controls to combat soaring inflation and rising interest rates.

Prime Minister Pierre Trudeau and the Liberals campaigned aggressively against the PC policy: "Zap! You're frozen!" Trudeau shouted derisively from platforms across the country. Greatly aided by the disunity within the PC Party, the Liberals easily won re-election with a majority government.

Because of the lack of discipline shown by some important Conservatives who broke ranks on the policy, we will never know if Stanfield's wage and price control policy would have been successful on its own merits. However, I have learned that it will always be difficult to attract voters when you are asking them to feel some pain in order to solve a problem. They are not being asked to join an aspirational campaign. Rather, they are being asked to look into the mud. Most voters spend their life in some form of mud and are far more likely to respond to a positive or uplifting message than to one of self-sacrifice.

The PC Party repeated the same folly in 1980 when it ran on a platform that included a large increase in gasoline taxes ... and Pierre Trudeau's political career was briefly resurrected.

1990 AND 1995 ONTARIO PROVINCIAL ELECTIONS

In 1990, as Mike Harris's campaign manager for the Ontario provincial election, I had commissioned a large quantitative study from Allan Gregg at Decima Research. Mike was the newly elected leader of the provincial Progressive Conservative Party, and few Ontarians knew much about him. The PCs were in third place in the polls. I was desperate to know what policy positioning would help us to survive as a party or to improve our position in the impending election. I say improve, not win, because the research showed the NDP was in second place behind the Liberals. Our second-choice analysis of the voters showed that for every three votes that the Liberals could lose, two of them would go to the NDP and only one to us. We could never catch up, even if the Liberal vote collapsed. And if it collapsed, the NDP would form the government.

Gregg reported that the most effective positioning for Mike was to be a tax fighter. This was not the most important issue on voters' minds, but it was the most important position that Mike could "own" by himself. In addition, it was credible for him to take this position as he was a fiscal conservative who believed in smaller government and lower taxes.

Harris fought the campaign as the tax fighter and finished third. The NDP under Bob Rae won that election, and the Liberals placed second. The PC Party managed a slight increase in its seat count in the Ontario Legislature. In the short term, the 1990 policy positioning did not appear to have worked for us. But what the tax-fighter stance did for Mike Harris was to provide a foundation for his success in the next provincial election, five years later.

Well before the 1995 election, Mike defied conventional political wisdom by pre-releasing his platform, the Common Sense Revolution. It was eighteen months before the election. Many politicians are reluctant to release policies too far in advance for fear they will be attacked, mocked, or stolen by their opponents. Mike's platform used the key 1990 tax-fighter policies — lower personal and corporate taxes — as its base.

The Liberal party and its leader Lyn McLeod went into the 1995 election poised to defeat Rae's unpopular NDP government and win the election. Early in the campaign, it became evident to voters that McLeod did not have a real plan for the province. Voters wanting change shifted their attention to the one leader who seemed to have a plan — Mike Harris with his Common Sense Revolution. Harris won a majority government.

The 1995 election was a case where policy decided the outcome. The platform was not built on a grand inspirational vision but rather upon a return to basics: lower taxes and smaller government — which may be visionary to some conservatives, but is quite mundane to most of the general population.

1999 NEW BRUNSWICK PROVINCIAL ELECTION

In early 1999, Bernard Lord, the new leader of the Progressive Conservative Party of New Brunswick, and his chief strategist, David McLaughlin, asked me to provide research services and political advice in preparation for the provincial election expected later that year.

The PC Party had been in the political wilderness in New Brunswick since its leader, Premier Richard Hatfield, lost the 1987 election to the Liberals under Frank McKenna. Hatfield had become very unpopular because of scandals which, with a high time-for-a-change number, resulted in the Liberals winning every seat in the legislature. Observers said that McKenna ran a very good campaign but did not offer a vision to the voters. He did not need to.

Keeping a long-standing promise to serve only ten years, McKenna left office ten years to the day after becoming premier. When he left he was still highly popular. He was replaced first by an interim leader and then by Camille Thériault, who won a leadership convention in 1998. Despite underwhelming the voters, Thériault entered the 1999 provincial election campaign with a significant lead in the polls: Liberal support was just under 50 percent, and the time-for-a-change number was only 49 percent. The Liberals looked safe.

Lord, a young bilingual lawyer from Moncton, had won his party's leadership in 1997. He realized he would need to drive up the time-for-a-change number to have any chance of victory. He fashioned a platform that included twenty promises that he committed to fulfilling in two hundred days, perhaps borrowing from a campaign tactic used by U.S. congressional leader Newt Gingrich in 1994.

The only one of the twenty promises that generated any media attention was a commitment to end tolls on a newly completed section of the Trans-Canada Highway between Fredericton and Moncton.

This was no grand vision, but during the campaign, bolstered by the twenty promises and Lord's performance in the televised leaders' debate, the time-for-a-change number rose and crested at the 60 percent level on the last weekend of the election. Lord's Progressive Conservative Party won forty-four of fifty-two seats in the legislature on June 7, 1999.

2003 TORONTO MAYORAL ELECTION

The mayoral campaign in Toronto in 2003 provided an opportunity to watch the interaction of policy and vision. David Miller had made his reputation with the public by helping to expose a multi-million-dollar computer leasing scandal at Toronto City Hall. A deep vein of cronyism in municipal politics was brought to the surface by this scandal.

Miller asked me to manage his campaign. After much thought, and following up on a suggestion by Miller's executive assistant Bruce Scott, we settled on the slogan "For a Clean City." This was a dual-purpose message: first, to clean up the corruption at city hall, and second, to clean up the city physically, as most residents said Toronto was not as pristine in 2003 as it had been before the amalgamation of the city and suburbs in 1998. The previous mayor and council had cut back street-cleaning and other public services.

Today, Miller explains his reasons for running in 2003 in these words:

> I was running because of my deep belief in the potential for city government to positively affect people's lives — I was offended to my core by the corruption allowed under Mel [former mayor Mel Lastman], not just because it was wrong, but because running a government that acted that way wasted its potential to make changes that positively impacted people's lives, particularly the most vulnerable. This may not have been captured fully in the "for a clean city" slogan but it was clear to me! My vision was of an inclusive twenty-first century city, with an activist, well-run city government leading the way.

While this expansive statement of his vision was clear to David, it may not have been clear to many others. His campaign was the only one to take a position against the building of a bridge to the Toronto Islands' Billy Bishop Airport — a position that was simple and easy to understand. Most saw David's slogan, therefore, as presenting a vision of protecting Toronto's waterfront, while David saw it in a broader perspective. To him, all the backroom manoeuvring around the bridge smelled of corruption.

135

Miller's principled stand against the bridge captured the imagination of the voters more than we realized, even though the early waterfront radio ads tested just so-so in comparison to the anti-corruption ads. The research showed broad support for protecting the waterfront. While this stance was strongest in the downtown, it also resonated with residents in Scarborough and Etobicoke, two former boroughs that took pride in their lake waterfront.

The policy position against the bridge was made more effective for Miller because he was the only major candidate who opposed the bridge. I learned later that the late John Tory Sr., the father of our major opponent, John Tory, had urged his son on a number of occasions to oppose the bridge. However, candidate Tory felt that he had to support the downtown business community and the *Toronto Star*, both of which had clamoured for the convenience of a downtown airport. Many observers later believed that Tory's pro-bridge stance tilted the election to Miller.

While Miller presented a large number of policies that were formally documented in a thirty-two-page colour brochure, only the promise to stop the construction of a bridge to the Island Airport had any real impact. It resonated with voters because it was simple and was backed by a vision, although it could be argued that most voters thought the vision was the protection of the waterfront rather than Miller's vision of an activist, well-run, and honest city government. It is of note that this promise and Bernard Lord's promise to cancel road tolls in New Brunswick had one thing in common: both were easy for voters to understand and to remember when they went to the polls.

Bruce Carson, one of the best policy specialists that I have worked with, agrees: "I learned to make sure that whatever policies a leader espouses have to be ones that could be easily communicated and understood."

2010 AND 2014 TORONTO MAYORAL ELECTIONS

In 2010 my mayoral candidate, Joe Pantalone, produced the most thoughtful and well-researched policies. He finished third. In 2014 Olivia Chow produced the most thoughtful and well-researched policies. She finished third. Neither Rob Ford, the winner in 2010, nor John Tory, the winner in 2014, bothered to produce a pamphlet outlining their policy platforms.

In 2010 Rob Ford presented an image of a frugal person who would respect the taxpayers' wallets. This was consistent with his track record in ten years as a city councillor. He tapped into an anger and discontent with the municipal government that had peaked in the aftermath of a garbage strike in the summer of 2009. He was seen to represent the values of average Torontonians who wanted a mayor who would listen to them rather than to so-called experts or elites. Ford did not need any big idea, grand vision, or even policies. He simply ran on an endlessly repeated mantra of "Stop the Gravy Train."

In 2014, while John Tory did present a vision of "Smart Track," a transit system that would reduce congestion on the downtown subway system, the major reason for his election was the desire to get rid of Rob Ford and his brother Doug. The voters wanted change, and he looked like the best bet to defeat the Fords. He did not need detailed policies. And while some say that his vision of Smart Track helped in his victory, the transit plan had so many financial and operational holes in it that few have argued that it significantly influenced the outcome.

2015 FEDERAL ELECTION

The federal election in 2015 provided another case study in which to examine the roles of policy and vision. None of the parties offered any grand vision. However, each of the three main parties and its leader presented a number of policies in great detail. A review by the *National Post* found that each party offered roughly the same number of specific policies.

Policy Grouping	Conservative Party	Liberal Party	NDP
Economy, taxes, and pocketbook issues	25	20	24
Security and terrorism	8	3	5
Energy and the environment	5	11	8

Policy Grouping (cont'd. from previous page)	Conservative Party	Liberal Party	NDP
Infrastructure and transport	7	7	3
Foreign affairs and defence	6	8	4
Social issues	3	7	10
Democratic reform and governance	2	7	5
Justice	8	3	5
Aboriginal issues	4	6	5
Total Number of Policies/Promises	68	72	69

On the surface it would appear that, in general, policies taken as a total did not affect the outcome. Each party presented promises designed to gain support from its accessible pool of voters. But two specific policies appear to have helped decide the outcome, one proposed by the NDP and one by the Liberals.

Tom Mulcair and the NDP announced before the election was called that, despite their expensive policies to provide change for Canadians — universal day care, universal drug care, increased health-care transfers to the provinces, and other initiatives — they would balance their first budget.

On August 25 they once again announced their fiscal position and explicitly said that they would balance their first budget for 2016–17. Voters could not see how the NDP could balance the budget and, simultaneously, keep their promises to increase spending on new and enlarged programs. More damaging was the perception that a balanced budget did not acknowledge the desire for change that 71 percent of respondents told pollsters they wanted.

The outcome suffered by Mulcair and the NDP brings to mind this comment from Aneurin Bevan, the Welsh politician and champion of social justice, who said, "We know what happens to people who stay in the middle of the road. They get run down."

As described earlier in Chapter 1, the Liberals presented a set of policies that were consistent with their ambition to be seen as the party representing change. The Liberals made a conscious decision to run deficits for three years in order to spend $10 billion per year on infrastructure projects that would stimulate growth in the economy. This policy announcement was made on August 27, two days after the NDP had pledged to balance their first budget. It turned the campaign around for the Liberals. (And we must not forget the huge boost that Justin Trudeau gave his campaign by meeting and exceeding a low level of expectations, discussed in Chapter 2.)

The policies presented by the governing Conservatives were largely seen as recycled promises or actions taken by them while in power — income splitting, tax credits for families, reductions on some specific taxes on businesses, increases in the annual contribution allowed to tax-free savings accounts (TFSAs), and balancing the federal budget in the current year. The message these policies sent to voters was that re-electing the Conservatives would mean more of the same — staying the course. In the absence of any grand vision being offered, voters decided that the Conservatives would not satisfy their desire for change and voted to give the Liberals a majority government.

I included "values" in the title of this chapter, and to this point I have not discussed their role in election outcomes. Yet values do play a significant role. As noted, most campaigns are policy based with no grand visions. They are duelling platforms. How do voters decide which platform is the best? How did the voters in the federal election of 2015 decide among the seventy or so promises being made by each of the three major parties?

I do not intend to insult the intelligence of voters when I observe that most of them do not have the time, interest, or ability to understand the promises made by candidates to solve the complicated issues facing governments today. The issues are often so complex that only economists and government bureaucrats can really understand them.

So voters revert to making judgments based their sense of which candidate or party best embodies the values that they, the voters, admire or look for in their elected officials. They gain their appreciation of the values of the candidates through their policy positions and performance before and during elections.

In my experience, the following values motivate voters:

- Fairness
- Humility
- Civility
- Compassion
- Courage
- Straightforwardness
- Inclusiveness
- Tolerance

You may notice that honesty is not on my list. Respondents in focus groups and in surveys invariably say they want their politicians to be honest. However, they will vote for a politician they know has broken promises. I have come to regard desire for honesty as a politically correct response. What voter would ever tell a pollster that he or she does not want honesty in our politicians? But honesty does not appear to drive voter intention in any significant way.

Articles published shortly after the 2015 federal election provided a rationale for the Trudeau Liberal Party victory. In one analysis, Martin Goldfarb, pollster for Justin Trudeau's father in the 1970s, wrote that he believes the values driving the Liberal campaign and its policy choices secured Justin's victory. Trudeau was seen as representing a return to traditional Canadian values of economic equality, inclusivity, and "sunny" optimism.

Another article was by Jaime Watt, a well-known Conservative political communications professional and commentator. Unlike Martin Goldfarb, Jaime based his work on focus groups and quantitative research that his polling firm had conducted both before and shortly after the election. He reported that voters wanted a return to the values they believe have traditionally defined Canadian society: civility, kindness, inclusion, and collaboration.

Martin, Jaime, and I might differ on what traditional Canadian values are, but we agree that the perception of the values presented by the three leaders had a large impact on the outcome in 2015.

In my opinion, however, these values paled in importance next to the exceptionally high level of desire for change, and Trudeau and the Liberals were seen by most Canadian voters as the most credible agent of change.

I have never shared the cynicism that so many members of the media and the general public seem to harbour about the integrity and dedication of the women and men who run for elected office. With very few exceptions, the candidates I have worked with in the course of four decades have been highly honourable people with a genuine desire to serve their community, province, or country to the very best of their ability.

I have respected no one more than the late Robert Lorne Stanfield, the Progressive Conservative premier of Nova Scotia, who was elected national leader of the party in 1967. He served in that capacity until 1976 when he stepped down, having lost three elections to Pierre Trudeau — in 1968, 1972 (narrowly), and 1974. Stanfield may have lacked the charisma of Trudeau the Elder, but he had all the qualities Canadians hope for in their prime minister — intelligence, moderation, understanding of complex issues, political judgment, experience in running a successful administration, and the ability to inspire loyalty among his followers.

I was Bob Stanfield's last national director at PC headquarters in Ottawa. I saw a lot of him in that period, particularly in the months between the 1974 election and the leadership convention in February 1976 that chose Joe Clark to succeed him. Those were quiet months for both of us. We were just about the only people in the party who were not actively involved in a leadership campaign; instead, we focused on raising money for the party so that Stanfield could leave a clean ledger for the new leader.

My wife Carol and I got to know Stanfield better during that period. His wife Mary was very ill and spent the last weeks of her life in the Ottawa Civic Hospital, just two blocks from our home. We invited him to drop by for a late supper on a number of evenings after visiting hours were over. I got to understand the life of a political leader a little better during those suppers. I recall at one point saying that he must have a large number of friends. He corrected me and said, "I have lots of acquaintances, but just a few friends — and my best friend is my wife." I thought to myself that being at the top of a political organization exacts its pound of flesh from leaders in many ways.

On a fairly regular basis I would receive a phone call from him near the end of the fiscal quarter. He wanted to take me to lunch. I quickly learned what that meant. He had not spent his quarterly minimum that was required at the Rideau Club, and, being a frugal sort, he wanted to make sure he used it all up. Regardless of motive, it was always a treat to spend time with him.

Sometimes we would discuss policy over lunch. I asked one day how, when he was premier of Nova Scotia, he was able to keep the size of government under control. He surprised me with a simple solution. He said that, as premier, he had retained the responsibility for the capital

The best prime minister Canada never had. This photo shows me with Robert Stanfield, who is signing campaign material for voters in Calgary during the 1974 federal election.

spending budget of the Nova Scotia government. That included funds for offices. He said the bureaucrats were forever asking for more space. But if they could not get it, they would not hire more staff. By keeping control of the capital budget, he was able to manage the size of government.

I also asked him how as national leader he managed issues in caucus when there were strongly held polar opposite views, with no obvious room for compromise. Capital punishment and abortion were two such issues that came his way. He replied that it was important to push people to acknowledge respect for the other side's position. He said if you could obtain agreement for people to respect one another's views, it was usually possible to obtain agreement to move forward on some aspect of the issue.

These fairly simple approaches to policy may be just another reason why many Canadians have described Stanfield as the best prime minister we never had.

Having settled on its vision and policies for a campaign, an organization needs to turn its attention to communicating its platform. The next three chapters will look at the all-important issue of communications from three different angles: the operation of the party nerve centre, commonly known as the "war room"; the use of social media; and the positives (or not) of negative advertising.

Chapter 8

The War Room

You can't fight in here. This is the War Room.
— PETER SELLERS as
President Merkin Muffley, *Dr. Strangelove*

The term *war room* was introduced to North American political vernacular by Democratic campaign manager James Carville for the 1992 Bill Clinton presidential campaign. In a nutshell, a war room is the command centre where a candidate's strategists and media officers work around the clock to respond quickly to attacks by opponents and media requests for information or comments, while also gathering research to mount offensives against all opponents.

The Carville war room was one campaign manager's organizational response to the challenges created by the era of instant communications and 24/7 media coverage. Carville recognized that campaigns needed a timely, organized approach to the constant stream of attacks and counterattacks.

In my first election campaigns in the early 1970s, communications were still in the Stone Age. Our leased Air Canada DC-9 transported a 200-pound telecopier machine from city to city so that the Conservative central speech-writing unit based in the Westbury Hotel in Toronto could send us the leader's speech for each evening's event.

Today the same speech could be sent via a hand-held BlackBerry or iPhone in nanoseconds; back then it took two to three minutes per page.

In the intervening years, the technology available to reporters covering elections has exploded. Pictures or videos can be captured on

Democratic Party guru and creator of the war room concept James Carville, with Stephen LeDrew of CP24, speaking at charity event in Toronto in 2012.

reporters' cell phones, and stories that could affect the campaign for better or ill can be shared around the clock on social media and the Internet.

The unrelenting pressure on candidates to be alert and to respond to breaking stories has increased exponentially in recent years. Keeping the candidate quickly informed is a job for the war room.

One might question whether a candidate should be judged on his or her ability to react quickly and effectively to a situation that has occurred 200 or 20,000 kilometres away. Some might argue that this is more a case of the media trying to play "gotcha" rather than as a means of evaluating important elements of leadership. Yet others believe a candidate's ability to deliver a quick response is a valid test of leadership ability. In my experience, the ability to react to fast-breaking events does matter, as it provides voters with an insight into candidates' unscripted reactions. An example from the 2014 Olivia Chow Toronto mayoral campaign illustrates that point.

At 2:00 p.m. on April 10, 2014, Olivia had just completed a round-table with Bay Street executives in Toronto's financial district and was meeting with the press to update them on her discussions with that group. Olivia was starting a scrum on the corner of York and Wellington Streets, just across the street from the storied Toronto Club.

The first question asked for her reaction to the death of federal finance minister Jim Flaherty. Reporters had just received this breaking news on their BlackBerrys and iPhones. Olivia was not aware of Jim's passing, but she made a moving expression of condolence for Jim's spouse, Christine Elliott, the deputy leader of the Ontario PC Party. It was very emotional and she put it in the context of her personal experience of having recently lost her own husband, Jack Layton, who was also an MP at the time of his death. It was one of Olivia's finest moments of the campaign.

The other pressure that has increased over the years is the need to quickly correct stories that are detrimental to a campaign, or to promote stories that may be helpful. In the era of instant communications, a campaign manager may have only minutes to get the message out.

Prior to 1992, the need for the functions of a war room existed, but the responsibilities were distributed among various individuals in the political organization. They included the campaign director, director of communications, press secretary, director of organization or director of research, or sometimes a group of individuals such as the policy committee or the campaign executive committee. This loosely structured method of dealing with rapid response seemed to suffice until the start of the era of 24/7 media and online coverage of politics.

I recall an example from 1986, when I was the campaign director for Gary Filmon and the Progressive Conservative Party of Manitoba, where a rapid response was required. I had been pressed into duty as campaign director on the day that Howard Pawley, the NDP Premier of Manitoba, called a provincial election. Filmon's campaign director resigned as a matter of personal protest after he failed to receive a patronage appointment that he expected from the Mulroney federal government. He had been Mulroney's chairman of organization for Manitoba in 1984, and he thought by 1986 he should have received his sinecure. I happened to be in Winnipeg that day meeting with Filmon about potential research for the party when the surprise election call was made. Gary asked me to stay and direct the campaign.

We arranged to place a glossy insert in the Saturday edition of the *Winnipeg Free Press* the weekend before voting day. We spent a lot of time getting the content right and getting it to the printers on schedule. Then on the Friday before it was to appear in the paper, someone came to me in the campaign office with a look of horror on his face. The printing of 125,000 inserts had been completed and he had just picked up some samples of the publication to bring to headquarters. The content had been rigorously vetted and approved, but for some reason the picture on the front of the publication had not been. There was Gary Filmon meeting a voter and standing beside one of our candidates — a man who had died months before. Worse, he had been a very high profile member of the Conservative caucus. We should have known.

What to do?

This was our major communications piece for the campaign, and there was no time (or money) to reprint it.

I had several hurried discussions with campaign staff. Someone came up with the approach that, in order to keep the issue quiet, we should have the leader call the candidate's widow and explain our mistake so

Dotting the I's and crossing the T's does matter. This campaign ad, designed for the 1986 provincial election for Gary Filmon's Manitoba PC Party, inadvertently showed Filmon and a deceased candidate.

that the family would not be surprised the next day. Gary, who was very concerned about the family's reaction, called, gave his explanation, and concluded by saying that her husband, who was deputy leader of the caucus at the time of his death, was the right person to be in the picture as he had been such a valued member of the team. The leader hoped the widow would understand.

As a result, the embarrassing gaffe never made it into the media.

Another rapid response was crafted in 1983 during John Crosbie's campaign for the national leadership of the Progressive Conservative Party. Whereas in the Filmon campaign we were trying to deal with a potentially negative situation, with Crosbie we were trying to take advantage of something positive. During the press conference in Toronto launching his leadership bid, John had candidly admitted that some of his advisers had been urging him to tone down his use of humour and present himself as a more serious candidate during the leadership process. After all, Crosbie was well known as a witty speaker, but not necessarily as a potential leader. He said that he was accepting the advice and continued, "I am going to go through this campaign looking like I was weaned on a pickle." With those few short words John hung a lantern on one of his potential shortcomings and dismissed it. Few ever accused him again of being a joker and not a serious candidate. Over time, John's performance at that convention and later as a prominent member of the Mulroney government put an end to the Newfie jokes that were prevalent in Canada in those days.

Someone in the communications group suggested that we build on this. A few days later one hundred white T-shirts arrived at campaign headquarters with a green pickle on the front. The shirts proudly worn by campaign staff helped us to demonstrate to all those watching that the joke was part of our strategy. The beauty of the pickle was that it allowed John to continue to be funny, but it removed the negatives generally associated with his use of humour.

I have worked with two of Canada's better known war room managers: Paul Rhodes, a Progressive Conservative, in the 2007 Ontario provincial election, and Warren Kinsella, a Liberal, in the 2014 Olivia Chow mayoral campaign.

Paul, a former reporter for CTV in Kitchener, Ontario, was the campaign communications director for the Ontario PC Party in the 1995, 1999, and 2003 provincial election campaigns.

In the 1993 federal election, Kim Campbell, the new PC leader, had led her party to a humiliating defeat. The party went from a majority government to two seats in the House of Commons. Though I was not directly involved with the federal election, I decided that a post-mortem of that campaign would be a useful exercise for the Ontario party and Mike Harris in planning for the upcoming 1995 Ontario provincial election campaign. In late November 1993 I assembled a group of twenty men and women who had been associated with Mike Harris in the past and who had been involved in the recent federal election. We met in the celebrated Albany Club in Toronto, where Conservatives go to drink, dine, plan, and plot.

The Liberals and the Conservatives had each developed war rooms for the 1993 federal election based on the 1988 Clinton model. Our review concluded that although the PC war room was well managed and had produced some excellent materials, the Liberal war room was much more responsive in its decision making. There were about four steps in the PC chain between the war room and the leader, making it difficult to get quick decisions on breaking issues. For the first time I realized that key decision makers had to be close to, or in, the war room.

Paul Rhodes recalls managing a group called "the bullpen" in the 1995–2003 period for the Ontario Tories. Paul describes the elements for operating a successful bullpen:

> It is important to have the right people in the room at the right time and keep others, who should not be there, out of the room. It is important where people meet. Everyone needs to be on call and available to discuss the next breaking issue. There needs to be an absence of hierarchy around the table. The research databases and researchers need to be close by, but not necessarily in, the room for the discussions.

He cited two examples of the bullpen's work during the 1995 Ontario provincial election campaign that elected Mike Harris premier of Ontario (which I discussed briefly in Chapter 7).

The Harris campaign released an economic statement late one afternoon. Within hours someone noticed that the statement included a number of factual errors. Paul and others worked late into the night to correct the document and went to the effort of putting corrected versions under the doors of all of the media travelling on the bus with the Harris campaign. The reaction from the media was positive. The Harris team was credited with finding the errors, owning up to them, and fixing them quickly.

In a situation similar to the Crosbie green pickle episode, Rhodes remembers the day during the 1995 election when Liberal leader Lyn McLeod said to the media that "tax cuts are wacky." Mike Harris was running on a platform called the Common Sense Revolution, which had personal income tax cuts for Ontarians as a major component. They also had polling that showed most voters liked the idea of tax cuts. Whether voters actually believed that politicians would deliver on a promise to reduce taxes was another matter.

Within hours Paul had T-shirts produced for all the campaign staff on the bus. The message on the shirts was "Call Me Wacky. I'm For Tax Cuts." The media reacted positively to this timely response to an opponent's attack. Mike Harris went on to win that election and become the twenty-second premier of Ontario.

I first worked with Paul in the 2007 provincial election. John Tory and I asked him to be director of communications and head of the war room for the Conservative campaign (which I discuss from different perspectives in Chapters 6 and 12).

Paul seized on newly available technology in 2007. He had a Bluetooth phone headset that he wore constantly, and he spent his time wandering around the campaign office looking as if he was talking to himself. In fact, he was constantly talking with candidates, campaign staff, or media.

In 2007, rather than having one separate room for the bullpen personnel, we had one empty space in the middle of the open campaign headquarters that contained a large table and ten or twelve chairs. My desk and those of the other members of the bullpen were located close to the empty table. When an issue arose we all left what we were doing and met at the table to respond to the new situation.

The atmosphere of a war room or bullpen is similar that of a media newsroom. The place is loud with many distractions, time pressure, stress, and an energy level that goes off the charts.

Seven years later, in 2014, I went looking for a war room manager for the Olivia Chow mayoral campaign. (You can find my reflections on this campaign scattered throughout this book, including Chapters 2, 4, and 6.) Warren Kinsella, a well-known backroom Liberal operative, may have seemed an unlikely choice to help me run a campaign for a well-known NDP politician. To some, it may have seemed an improbable Grit-Tory marriage of convenience.

There was a simple reason for my choice, however. Warren had approached Olivia in 2013 and said that he had been impressed by her work in Ottawa on behalf of David Chen, the owner of a grocery store called the Lucky Moose in Olivia's federal riding of Trinity-Spadina. Chen had been arrested for catching and detaining a shoplifter who had stolen food from his store. Olivia stood up for David when he was charged with assault and forcible confinement when all he was doing was defending his shop. She submitted proposals in the House of Commons to loosen the law related to citizens' arrests. With all-party support, the law was changed by the Harper Conservative government, and Chen was acquitted. (In one of my disappointing moments in politics, I watched in September 2014 as David Chen stood in front of a bank of microphones endorsing John Tory for mayor of Toronto, because he thought small business would be better supported by Tory. A fine way to thank the person who had kept him out of jail!

Back to the war room. We had a number of discussions about how to utilize Warren's talents. He had earned the reputation of being a polarizing figure in both the federal and Ontario Liberal parties. He was not liked by the Paul Martin Liberals or by Kathleen Wynne's provincial Liberals because he had been a fierce Jean Chrétien loyalist, and in 2013 he had supported Sandra Pupatello for the leadership of the Ontario party in preference to Wynne.

In the Chow organization we took the approach that members of all political parties were welcome, and we needed some Liberals on our team. We had approached a number of them, but none were enthusiastic about helping a high-profile New Democrat become mayor of Toronto. After all, Olivia and Jack Layton had played a huge role in the defeat and humiliation of the Liberals in the 2011 federal election. Many Liberals saw nothing positive in helping to make Olivia mayor of Toronto.

I asked some of these Liberals about using Warren Kinsella in our campaign. They said he would drive other Liberals away. We eventually decided to use him for two simple reasons: there were no other Liberals clamouring to join us, and Kinsella in my opinion was the best person for the job we wanted done.

In 2007 Warren had written a book titled *War Room,* in which he claimed that "the best war rooms ... attract attention, they reach inside people's hearts and minds and they change outcomes."

I have a simpler standard for a war room: a war room should accentuate the positives and try to eliminate the negatives — quickly. And that is what Kinsella brought to the Chow campaign. While we needed a war room during the latter half of 2013, the election laws of the City of Toronto prohibited us from spending any money until Olivia had registered as a candidate at some point after January 1, 2014. So Warren offered to be an unpaid volunteer on the Chow campaign, and he set out to recruit a number of young people to work as volunteers, too. They started work immediately. Because we were barred temporarily from spending to rent office space, they worked online.

Regular morning conference calls were initiated and responsibilities divided up. Each person was assigned to monitor an individual mayoral opponent or daily media coverage, or to report on developments in specific topics or issues. I believe this was the first online war room ever created. It was only partway through the 2014 campaign that I got to meet these young people face to face. They all worked on their assignments from their offices and homes, very often while most of the world was sleeping.

On a campaign organization chart, the head of the war room reports to the campaign director or to the director of communications, or to both.

In practice, the daily schedule of Olivia Chow campaign meetings looked like this:

- 8:00 a.m.: The war room meets by teleconference — chaired by the war room manager

  Agenda:
  ○ Review of daily media monitoring — determine follow-up required (if any)
  ○ Review each opponent's previous day's activities
  ○ Report on activities planned by opponents for current day and determine actions required
  ○ General discussion and summarize plans for today

- 8:30 a.m.: The campaign operations group meets by teleconference — chaired by the campaign director: the war room manager reports the results of the 8:00 call, and actions discussed by the war room are conveyed to the operations group and responsibilities for today's plans coordinated

While the agenda for each day's war room meeting was standard, the outcomes of each meeting were not standard and were dependent to a large extent on media stories and the plans and activities of our opponents. Then there were days where we had an event or announcement planned.

Generally, when we were playing defence and responding to a media story or planned events or announcements by opponents, there were a number of options open to us:

- Quickly respond to a negative story using our candidate, campaign spokesperson, or third-party supporter to get out our side of the story or our explanation

- Change the channel on the story by offering a new angle or a competing story to reduce the media's interest in the initial story
- Blunt the effect of a planned announcement by an opponent by providing media personnel with background information designed to reduce its impact, by questioning the initiative or by outlining negative consequences of the action
- Find a way to get our candidate into the opponent's story, if it will be helpful

When we were playing offence, the war room developed plans to enhance our announcements. These plans could include any of the following:

- Identify third-party spokespersons to the media and prepare speaking notes for their use
- Provide background papers for the announcement or event for use by the media (provide one selected media outlet with advance notice of the occasion; attempt to get early-morning radio or print coverage on the day of the event)
- Provide an interesting visual backdrop for the event to ensure good television coverage

In the normal course of events, the campaign director and the head of the war room are in sync with the actions being planned by the war room. However, nothing was normal when it came to working with Warren Kinsella. He had offered to help Olivia because he respected her track record of helping people such as David Chen. But he was also driven by animosity toward John Tory. In *War Room*, he describes "the despicable ads" that Tory, as Kim Campbell's campaign manager, had run against his mentor Jean Chrétien, the Liberal leader, in the 1993 federal election.

Eventually, Warren's emotions got the better of him and he put out a tweet that suggested that John Tory's "Smart Track" transit plan was segregationist because it did not include service to such low-income and highly diversified areas of Toronto, such as Jane-Finch and Rexdale. Tory then attacked Chow for playing dirty politics and called upon Chow to get rid of "volunteer" Kinsella. Warren withdrew the tweet and apologized. But the situation spun out of control and eventually led to a parting of the ways between Kinsella and the Chow campaign.

In my opinion, Warren was embarrassed and upset that Tory had gotten the better of him and that he had allowed himself to become something that successful war room managers never do: that is, to make themselves an issue in the campaign. The timing of his tweet could not have been worse for Chow. It occurred just at the end of two good weeks of announcements and debate performances by Olivia, and it blunted any chance she had to move back up in the polls.

Whether it is called a war room, a bullpen or a rapid-response group, a formalized unit under the direction of a senior operative who reports to the campaign director is an essential ingredient for political success today when competition for airtime, print space, and social-media presence is so very intense.

A successful war room is one that has imagination, is served well by research, has good relations with the media, has a lack of hierarchy, and, above all, is fast-acting because it has the decision makers in the room.

Robin Sears is an extremely talented political operative whom I have had the pleasure of working with and against over the years. In my opinion he is the best rapid-response person in Canada. A New Democrat, Robin works for both political and non-political clients.

During the 2015 federal campaign Robin observed that the definition of a war room was being stretched. Whereas the war room used to encompass only rapid response, it now included virtually all of the functions of a campaign, including research.

He says it used to be possible for campaigns to plan messages for a twenty-four-hour news cycle. Today the job of message control has been made much more difficult for two reasons. First, the speed of online communications has increased; and second, the number of journalists who travel with party leaders during campaigns has shrunk. Reporters have learned that with online access to information they do not really need to leave their offices to write a story. What is more, news organizations feel that parties charge far too much money for seats on their campaign planes in an age when traditional media revenues are a fraction of what they once were.

Sears observed that the *Toronto Star*, the country's largest newspaper, had not put a reporter on the road with any party leader for the first month of the 2015 campaign, and even in the dying days of the campaign the number of journalists travelling with party leaders was at an all-time low. How, he asked, can a campaign hope to control the message in the all-important daily news cycles when it has little or no face-to-face time with the media?

Bret Snider, a long-time PC Party activist from Toronto, is not a fan of war rooms. "The war room is a shallow campaign response to the 24/7 news cycle and, most recently, its evil sister, social media, that demands a response but for no good reason," he says. "It is the fast food of debate, reasoned thought, and discourse. It is not tempered or considered. It is reactive."

I too wonder whether the "war room" nomenclature has not contributed to the decrease in civility and decorum in politics today. Donald Trump, campaigning for the 2016 Republican presidential primary, described his campaign as a war against two enemies, Hillary Clinton, a Democrat, and Jeb Bush, a fellow Republican.

None of this can be helpful for democracy.

Perhaps my small contribution to this concern might be to rename this function in my next campaign as "the rapid response group" or "bullpen 2.0."

Regardless of what it is called, from my vantage point the war room — or centralized rapid response group — is essential for quick response and attack capabilities in this 24/7 communications environment.

A successful war room depends upon having quality research, smart and imaginative people, and an effective social-media strategy. The next chapter will examine the lessons that I have learned about social media and the positive, and not so positive, roles that it plays in today's politics.

Chapter 9

The Power of Social Media

What is interesting is the power and the impact of social media. So we must try to use it in a good way.
— MALALA YOUSAFZAI

If your music is good, you will have fans, not because you have spent time chatting on social media.
— BRYAN ADAMS

In my world, the ad industry, the importance of social media is accepted for a traditional reason: reach. Facebook is as big as the traditional broadcast networks combined. It is widely accepted in the communications industry that it is a valuable channel.
— PATRICK THOBURN, founder of Matchstick,
a Toronto-based social-media marketing agency

Much has been written about how social media has influenced politics. However, it should be stressed that social media is just one part of digital communications. The Internet, email, and data are the others. And each of these has also fundamentally changed the way in which politics is conducted today.

I have only used social media in my more recent campaigns, but I have come to understand its role, its limitations, and its impact, both good and bad, on politics. Whatever we think of it, social media is here to stay, and as Malala Yousafzai says, we need to learn how to use it in a good and effective manner. I have learned, just as Bryan Adams did, that winning the social-media metrics battle — having the largest number of Facebook fans, Twitter followers, or LinkedIn connections — has little impact, whether you're talking about the number of discs sold or the votes gained on election day. As with all other tools in the campaign manager's kit, social media performs a supporting role; the candidate is the main actor, and it is his or her performance that will, in most cases, ultimately determine success. It is for this reason that professional social-media planners refer to the number of followers and fans and connections as "vanity" metrics. They look good but have little real influence on the number of sales or votes generated.

In the end, social media is just another communications vehicle, and while it does offer more connectivity and interaction than other vehicles, the same basic first principles governing the effectiveness of communications seem to apply to social media.

In order to be effective, a message needs to get noticed, be relevant, and usually be brief. The message needs to be easy to understand and remember. I vividly recall attending a presentation in the mid-1970s by a speechwriter and communications expert who worked for former prime minister Pierre Trudeau. He suggested that everything in life has three components, and that fact should be kept in mind when preparing a speech or a presentation. He offered as proof that a book has a beginning, a middle, and an ending. He said that in religion there is Father, Son, and Holy Ghost, and nobody remembers the Ten Commandments. The fact that I remember the message and not the name of the presenter reinforces the message he was communicating that day. If you give people too much to absorb they are overwhelmed and may not remember the important points that you would like them to remember.

Not only should messages be brief — they should, if possible, be accompanied by an image. The old adage that a picture is worth a thousand words applies more today than ever before; messages are most effective if they are posted with a visual or video.

* * *

In general, digital communication has significantly affected the cost side of many of the functions of a campaign. Candidates are now able to do each of the following at a significantly reduced cost:

- Communicate directly with voters with customized messages (based upon data mining)
- Distribute campaign ads or videos on YouTube
- Recruit volunteers for the campaign organization
- Allow for like-minded voters and activists to easily share news and information about campaign events or policy announcements
- Raise funds (through the use of "money bombs": "We need to raise $10,000 in the next two days to help pay for the next round of television ads")
- Obtain feedback from the public on policy or breaking news

All of the above can be done without spending a dime, other than paying the salaries of workers who specialize in digital communications.

Some might wonder why an entire campaign could not be run exclusively with digital communications at a significantly reduced cost. The reason is that there is significant competition for exposure on these sites. While Facebook postings may be noticed by thousands of voters and forwarded to thousands of others, they may also be ignored. A good video may go viral on YouTube, but it may also be ignored. For now, at least, campaign managers will be forced to use paid media to get their messages and ads out until they learn the foolproof secret to generating viral distribution of their online postings. A number of the social-media networks now offer paid media options for advertisers. Ads can be purchased on Facebook, YouTube, and a number of other sites.

Not only do sites such as Facebook, YouTube, and others offer political organizers a great way to spread the message about the candidates and parties they are working for, they also offer a treasure trove of data (Big Data) that organizations, including political campaigns, can use to better understand the makeup and interests of potential voters. The advent of the use of Big Data has allowed organizations and political candidates to customize their messages to potential customers or voters.

Big Data is a term that describes the large volume of data — both structured and unstructured — that inundates a business or a campaign on a day-to-day basis. It is not the amount of data that is important, however. It's what organizations do with the data that matters. Big Data can be analyzed for insights that lead to better decisions and strategies for both businesses and political campaigns.

I read with interest of how data-driven decision making played an important role in Barack Obama's re-election campaign in 2012. The campaign team employed dozens of data crunchers who collected every bit of data they could find. They noticed, for instance, that actor George Clooney had a great appeal with West Coast females, aged forty to forty-nine. These women were the single most likely group to hand over cash for a chance to dine in Hollywood with Clooney and Obama. A contest was launched and succeeded in raising millions.

Later in the election, the campaign sought out an East Coast celebrity who had similar appeal with the same demographic. They chose Sarah Jessica Parker. The next Dinner with Barack Obama contest was born: a chance to eat at Parker's West Village brownstone.

Political parties in Canada have started to embrace the concepts of using Big Data, and this was evident during the 2015 federal election. As candidates left the doors of voters, the information they gleaned from their conversations was entered into an iPad or scribbled into a notebook. It eventually wound up in a large database of that political party.

The parties use software to analyze the data gathered to help them plan their campaigns. The Liberal Party of Canada's software is called Liberalist, and the accompanying app is MiniVAN. The Conservatives have CIMS with a mobile version called C2G. The NDP has Populus, a smaller version of campaign analytics. The parties use the analytics obtained to micro-target voters to get out the vote, recruit volunteers, and identify donors.

Party officials defend the use of large databanks. They say they are not creating secret files, but rather using a method that lets them understand what voters are talking about and their concerns. But analytics is much more than that. It uses algorithms, a.k.a. mathematical equations, to segment voters into groups such as hard and soft supporters, and to determine what issues concern them. The parties can then target them with specific messages in order to gain their support.

The following example, reported during the 2015 federal election by a CBC reporter, illustrates how Big Data can be used.

Stella Ambler, a young volunteer who had worked with me on several Ontario PC campaigns, was elected as a Conservative MP in 2011. The CBC accompanied her on her door-to-door canvassing in 2015 in the riding of Mississauga-Lakeshore.

The CBC reported the following:

> While canvassing recently in Mississauga-Lakeshore, one of Canada's 30 new ridings, Conservative incumbent Stella Ambler met Alan, a homeowner, at his front door. Alan is friendly but not currently supporting the Conservatives, saying he doesn't like their record on the environment.
>
> Ambler politely listens, hoping he is a voter she can persuade in the future. The information he gives her is documented by Ambler's patient campaign assistant.
>
> "It goes into a database, and we'll be able to generate lists," Ambler explains, leaving Alan's doorstep.
>
> "Alan here will be on the list of people who care about the environment. So let's say the prime minister makes an announcement about the environment. We'll make sure we tell Alan."

(The data manipulation did not help Stella Ambler. She was defeated in Mississauga-Lakeshore on October 19 by Liberal Sven Spengemann.)

While the use of Big Data is having an impact on the ability of organizations to customize their messages to their target audiences and affect the behaviour of those audiences, the users of social media are also exerting a powerful influence over society in general, and politics in specific.

Consider the latest American statistics from PEW Research:

- Thirty-nine percent of American adults have engaged in one of eight civic or political activities with social media. Promoting material related to politics, encouraging people to vote, and posting their own thoughts or comments on political or social issues were the most reported activities.
- In the 2012 presidential election, 55 percent of all registered voters went online to watch video news reports about the election, to watch previously recorded videos of candidate speeches, press conferences, or debates, or to watch informational videos that explained political issues. These were the most reported activities. It is worth noting that each of these top three activities involved the use of video.

There have been numerous studies on the effects of social-media sites on offline behaviour. Shelley Boulianne, of MacEwan University in Edmonton, conducted a review of thirty-six such studies in 2015 and has concluded that "the greater use of social media did not affect people's likelihood of voting or participating in a campaign."

Some researchers explain this by saying that the participation on social-networking sites seems to satisfy many individuals' need for electoral participation.

POLITICAL CAMPAIGNS AND SOCIAL MEDIA

When I first encountered the use of social media in political campaigns, I had little or no expectation of what its impact would be for our campaigns. It would be some time before I began to get a better understanding of that. It happened during my first exposure to digital communications in politics of any real consequence, the 2006 David Miller mayoral campaign.

I had recruited Patrick Thoburn, a young entrepreneur, to work as a volunteer on David's campaign. Patrick was the founder of Matchstick, a Toronto-based social-media marketing agency that today builds social brands, that part of the brand that deals with customer interactions.

I had met Patrick a few years earlier when our research firm conducted a ground-breaking study for his firm on media consumption by teenagers. I remember that one of the conclusions of the research was that young people would no longer be watching and using television as their major source of information. Another conclusion was that radio would still be important because it could be listened to at the same time that young people were on social-networking sites. I recall some mainstream media saying "no way" when they saw these results. Recent history has proved Patrick correct. I did not know what Patrick could contribute to our campaign in 2006, but he was bright and would bring what he could from his new world of digital communications.

Using an early form of social media, we put together a friend-to-friend fundraising campaign for David Miller. I understand this was one of the first, if not the first, fundraising campaign for a Canadian political campaign that aimed to leverage the personal social networks of supporters. This was pre-Facebook and pre-Twitter. We learned that most of our supporters — even the most loyal — were reluctant to solicit funds from their personal networks over the Internet, though they were very obliging in making personal contributions via email. (In 2006 just 10 percent of our total campaign donations came from our online efforts.)

I understand that "peer-to-peer fundraising" by political campaigns is rarely used today because of the same reluctance we encountered. This is an example of one of the limitations of social media.

In 2010, for the Joe Pantalone mayoral campaign, we used only email for fundraising. Joe had few address files to work with, and, as I recall, again just 10 percent of the funds we raised came from our online efforts. That said, Joe's track record over the years as city councillor and deputy mayor under David Miller allowed us to raise sufficient funds through the events we held to finish the campaign with a balanced budget.

Much of what I have learned about social media comes from my more recent experience with the 2014 Olivia Chow Toronto mayoral campaign. The social-media plan for the Olivia Chow campaign centred upon three areas:

- Communications

  - Create our own message
  - Frame the message
  - Influence journalists, politicos, bloggers, and leaders
  - Be part of the conversation

- Organization

  - Build momentum
  - Recruit volunteers, supporters, and voters
  - Move supporters up the ladder of engagement

- Fundraising

  - Raise money
  - Raise more money

Our digital director on the campaign was Jennifer Hollett, who more recently was an NDP candidate in Toronto in the 2015 federal election. In training sessions, Jennifer uses a simple chart to explain various social-networking sites and their uses to social-media neophytes like myself.

- Twitter — I'm eating a #donut
- Facebook — I like donuts
- Foursquare — This is where I eat donuts
- Instagram — Here's a vintage photo of my donut
- YouTube — Here I am eating my donut
- LinkedIn — My skills include donut eating
- Pinterest — Here's a donut recipe

- LastFM — Now listening to "Donuts"
- G+ — I'm a Google employee who eats donuts

Needless to say, social media is constantly evolving, and a number of these platform references are already dated. Campaign managers need to keep that in mind and be aware of and make use of current popular social-media sites when developing their strategic plans. Every campaign needs to start with an overall strategic plan. Each function of the campaign requires a plan that is consistent with that overall strategy, and digital communications is no exception. A strategy for email, Internet, and social media is required together with the tactics that will be employed to achieve the desired results.

Many organizations have experts more knowledgeable than I am in this sphere. I cannot provide the depth of information that professionals have at their fingertips when they sit down to create a plan for an organization or a campaign. But I will try to give a taste of what social-media planners need to consider in order to select the most effective platforms for their client or candidate.

Everyone is on Facebook — over twenty million individuals in Canada. Because of this reach, political candidates usually decide that they too have to be on Facebook.

While most people consider YouTube to be the home of online video, in August 2014 Facebook passed YouTube in total number of desktop video views after it introduced a new feature that allowed it to compete more effectively with YouTube. However, YouTube continues to be an effective vehicle to reach voters and opinion leaders. All political campaigns need to use it.

During the initial stages of the 2010 Toronto mayoral race, I attended a meeting of the fledgling Adam Giambrone for Mayor Campaign committee. Adam was my client. We had decided to whet the appetite of opinion leaders and voters prior to his official campaign launch by releasing a humorous video depicting Adam training to be a candidate — shaking hands, doing pushups, and running on the spot. The video culminated in Adam running up a set of stairs in downtown Toronto accompanied by the music for the first *Rocky* film, emulating Sylvester

Stallone's run up the Philadelphia Museum steps in the epic Hollywood sports-drama movie.

Ten minutes after releasing the video on YouTube, almost all of the BlackBerrys in our meeting started to buzz. While we got immediate attention, much of the reaction was not favourable. Many viewers thought the image portrayed of Adam was not consistent with what they were looking for in a candidate for the serious job of mayor. It was a slight blow to the campaign. A much bigger blow was soon to follow, and Adam's campaign came to a screeching halt one week later as he exited the race amidst a sex scandal.

There are five million Twitter accounts in Canada, significantly fewer than Facebook. However, most journalists and opinion influencers are there, making Twitter a "must" site for candidates and their war rooms.

New sites are constantly being developed. One that has become popular is Instagram, an app that lets users post and share photos or visuals. Because it is new, a candidate's use of this site signals that he or she is in the forefront of the use of social media.

Local differences may influence which sites a candidate uses. For example, certain cities may have disproportionately higher than average level of Twitter activity.

Jennifer Hollett's overall approach is to get people who use social media to go offline (for example, to come to an event or make a donation), and to use their favourite sites to encourage their friends to join them at the event or to volunteer or donate.

She describes her desired digital ladder of engagement. The easiest thing is to convince someone to become a Facebook fan or Twitter follower, or to sign up to receive information emails from a campaign. The list that follows is in increasing order of engagement. The objective is to get people to move down the list and up the ladder of engagement.

- Becoming a Facebook "like" or Twitter follower, or signing up to an email list
- Sharing content with others on social media, filling out a survey online, pledging to vote
- Donating to the campaign

- Attending an event — fundraiser, volunteer training; dropping by the office; having a one-on-one meeting with the candidate
- Participating in canvassing or a phone bank, or volunteering at the office
- Leading a canvass or phone bank, hosting a fundraiser

I have much to say in this book about the 2014 Toronto mayoral campaign — see, for example, the discussions in Chapters 1, 4, 6, and 8. John Tory won that campaign. His digital media presence, or participation, appears to have had little to do with his win.

	Facebook fans at end of campaign	Twitter at end of campaign	Instagram posts at end of campaign	Votes on October 19, 2014
Olivia Chow	66,000	61,100	2,700	226.879
John Tory	12,000	35,400	1,670	394,775
Doug Ford	10,000	3,600	400	330,610

Political observers in Toronto in 2014 thought that David Soknacki, a former city budget chief, had by far the best social-media presence in the mayoral contest. He was seen to be edgy and innovative. David withdrew from the race two months before election day when the polls told him he could not obtain more than 2 to 3 percent voter support in a five-person race. This is one more demonstration of the lack of correlation between online activity and electoral success.

The major value of social media in a political campaign is that it provides voters with direct access to politicians. It allows for conversation between candidates and the voters they are trying to win over. Therefore, wise candidates set aside time for these conversations.

Many candidates are afraid to participate on social media. Some do not understand the technology, while others fear posting something that will come back to bite them. The disqualification of twenty-one candidates from all three major parties in the 2015 federal election for something they had posted online in the past did little to calm those fears.

Others, like me, cannot really afford to spend the time necessary to participate in what is basically a conversation with anyone who wishes to establish contact. A candidate is really not in a position to delegate to a staffer the majority of his or her participation on sites such as Twitter and Facebook the way a business corporation can delegate much of this function to a firm such as Matchstick.

While many political observers in North America use Barack Obama as the poster child for use of social media, I have recently become interested in two Canadian politicians who are both known to be effective users of social media.

One is Naheed Nenshi, the mayor of Calgary. He is recognized for making extremely effective use of his Twitter account. He realizes there is nothing worse than a boring presence on social media. People want or expect him to be funny, irreverent, available, innovative, and relevant — in other words, they expect him to be himself.

He uses social media to inform his voters about what he is doing for them as mayor. As he travels across the city, he uses the Web to promote local community events and highlight citizens and groups that are doing great work in Calgary. He is even known to post messages about lost pets.

But he has also learned to deliver what social media wants. Consider the following two exchanges between Nenshi and members of the public.

One Twitter user tweets: "My limp dick could do a better job of running this city."

Nenshi: "Well, I am away for a few days, so tell him to give it a try! PS: Look into pharmaceuticals for the limpness issue."

Another Twitter user tweets: "What is the point of the ridiculously expensive bridge again? What does it signify?"

Nenshi: "I think it's to be used to cross the river."

Nenshi is visible to his Twitter followers and is seen to be doing his job. I would note that he has over 275,000 Twitter followers, while the daily circulation of the local newspaper, the *Calgary Herald,* is just 123,722.

The second Canadian politician I have in mind is Tony Clement, a Cabinet minister in the Stephen Harper government. While Tony sees the Internet and email as just as important as social media, he regards social-media sites as being fundamentally different. They provide for interaction and for far greater reach.

He notes the positive impact of social media in non-democratic countries where communities of belief have been created online to galvanize people into action. In democratic countries, he sees social media developing communities of common interest. He quotes the example of generating opposition to Bill C-51 — the Harper government's anti-terrorism legislation.

I was curious how such a busy politician could fit social media into his schedule. Tony says he has no block of time built into his daily agenda. He estimates that he spends one hour each day online, but it is in small chunks —a three-minute wait for a meeting to start, for example, or five minutes while driving to an event. He says that he resists going on social media at 3:00 a.m.: "That's when you are going to make a mistake." His participation on social media is something that cannot be delegated to staff. He credits his large following on Twitter to the authenticity of his participation.

Tony is frank in describing how he deals with social media. He admits to having to develop a thick skin as a result of the negative comments that sometimes get posted about him.

So why does he use social media? Clement says it gives him instant notification of breaking news, and he then has the opportunity to insert himself into the story. However, it appears that his main motivation is that social media provides him with "dimensionality." He is able to show his personality to the voters. "It allows me to use my passions — my constituency, my music, and my hockey team, the Montreal Canadiens."

He says he learned a lot during the 2015 federal election. The mainstream media still has an important role. He believes its coverage of the Senator Mike Duffy trial and the Syrian refugee crisis had a huge impact on the election outcome. "The value of social media, as compared to the mainstream media, has been overplayed by many people."

He is a heavy user of Twitter (56,000 followers) and a relatively light user of Facebook (just 600 Facebook fans), and has 5,600 Instagram followers. He knows that "influencers," especially journalists, are on Twitter, and that information they glean there very often finds its way to a larger audience in the mainstream media.

THE GOOD, THE BAD, AND THE UGLY

While my social-media campaign experience has been limited, I have learned some important lessons. Overall, social media has significantly affected each function in a political campaign. In some areas it has proved to be successful, in others less so. From my vantage point it seems that social media is most effective when used alongside more traditional tools. For example, social media should be used to complement, not replace, door-knocking by the candidate. Each campaign manager, therefore, needs to find a balance in his or her use of various tools. How many hours, for example, should the candidate spend meeting people online as opposed to meeting them in person at the door or in a shopping mall?

And candidates and campaign managers also need to learn to use social media effectively and appropriately.

I have observed the good, the bad, and the ugly with the use of social media in politics.

The Good
Social-media sites provide:

- An opportunity for more voters to get engaged in the political process
- A way for ignored or fringe candidates to get their message out
- A means for voters to connect directly to candidates and to converse with them
- A method by which candidates can get direct feedback from voters on issues and policies
- An inexpensive way for candidates to get ads, videos, images, and other assets into circulation

- A good vehicle to assist a candidate to build a campaign organization
- New methods for getting voters involved in campaigns
- A means by which a candidate can get his or her story out if it is not being covered by the mainstream media

The Bad

Social-media sites provide:

- A temptation to mainstream media to use unknown sources from social media for their stories or columns, with content that never gets verified
- "Lazy" journalists with an excuse not to have to talk to voters on the street, at their door, or in a shopping mall
- A narrowing of political views, or political polarization, that occurs among online participants: research has shown that users of Facebook and Twitter, as well as bloggers, tend to engage almost exclusively with people who share their political views
- The potential for candidates to post something online that can be embarrassing or potentially fatal for their campaigns
- A risk that a candidate or campaign may devote too much attention to this new tool and not enough time to the more demanding and less glamourous forms of campaign activity, such as door knocking

The Ugly

Social media sites provide:

- Information that destroyed the political futures of twenty-one candidates in the 2015 federal election; because of these "bozo" candidates, look for parties in future campaigns to spend a lot more time and effort on social-networking sites to discover information about their own candidates, as well as researching the flaws of their opponents

- Opportunity for just about anyone to post the most vile, obscene, and tasteless material without any consequences and without permitting the target of the attack any recourse; this happened on a regular basis during the Olivia Chow campaign, with racist and sexist comments appearing online
- Information that is changing what people want from their leaders: personality is becoming more important than image (a recent article in *POLITICO* magazine claims, "Social media favours the 'bitty' over the 'meaty,' the cutting over the considered, emotion over reason. The fiery populist now seems more desirable, more worthy of attention than the cool policy wonk. In the 2016 U.S. presidential primaries, the crusty Bernie Sanders and the caustic Donald Trump were much more likely to get hearted, hash-tagged, friended or followed")

Regardless, as I mentioned at the start of this chapter, the same basic first principles of successful communications apply to the use of social-media sites that once applied to fax machines, the buggy-whip version of digital communications.

The material posted has to be innovative, engaging, relevant, and credible to be effective with voters. This really forces candidates and campaign workers to be imaginative to get noticed.

Jennifer Hollett described for me how she organized two national leaders' debate-viewing parties during the 2015 federal election campaign. She posted a Facebook event for each party to watch the debates at a pub in her riding in downtown Toronto. No money was spent to "boost" the posts, and nothing else was done to promote the events. No emails, no phone calls — just friends inviting friends on Facebook. On each occasion, the bar was filled to fire-code capacity, and many new supporters became engaged in the offline operations of the campaign. She had built a strong enough Facebook community to move them from online to offline, moving them up the ladder of engagement. In addition, local TV camera crews showed up on both occasions.

Where does the use of social media go to from here in politics?

I suggest that the first principles of effective communications will continue to apply, regardless of the development of new sites and apps.

- Voters will always reward innovation and imagination.
- A picture will continue to be worth a thousand words, and the use of videos and photos on sites such as Instagram, Facebook, YouTube, and whatever the next vehicle may be, will assume even greater importance for the effective delivery of political messages.
- Because over 70 percent of the users of social-media sites want to receive material on their mobiles, short messages will continue to be needed to be read by, and have an impact on, the electorate.

As Bryan Adams said, good singers (and candidates) will be rewarded on their merits, regardless of the effectiveness of social media or any other campaign tool.

As a footnote to the 2015 federal election results, Jennifer Hollett finished a strong second on October 19. Despite running an excellent campaign, including her strong social-media effort, she lost to Justin Trudeau's star candidate, Chrystia Freeland, now the minister of international trade, proving once again that while social media is an excellent tool, it cannot guarantee electoral success.

* * *

I have already pointed out that one of the ugly sides of social media is that it provides anyone with the opportunity to post vile and obscene material online without permitting the target of the attack to respond.

What is the impact of that on a political candidate?

This broadens into a larger question about the impact of all negative attacks and especially negative advertising. How effective are attack ads in determining the outcome of elections? The next chapter will look at the lessons I have learned about the use of negative ads.

Chapter 10

Negative Advertising

Negative ads work, except when they don't.
— JOHN SIDES,
The Moneyball of Campaign Advertising

Negative ads — or "attack ads," as they are popularly known today — have been employed as weapons in American politics since the early years of the republic. Supporters of President John Quincy Adams used the "Coffin Handbills" in his bid for re-election in 1828. These were a series of twelve pamphlets that attacked his rival, Andrew Jackson. Jackson's mother was branded a prostitute and his wife an adulteress — and we think today's ads are tough! Adams's attack ads were tough, but they were not successful. Andrew Jackson won the presidency handily.

The first negative radio ads were used by the Republicans in 1936.

And there have been many famous, or notorious, negative television ads. One was the "Daisy" ad used by President Lyndon Johnson in 1964 against his Republican opponent Barry Goldwater. This ad raised the prospect of nuclear war occurring if the hawkish Goldwater were to be elected. It featured a nuclear countdown as a young girl plucked petals from a daisy. The ad only ran once, but it doomed Goldwater's chances.

The previously mentioned "Willie Horton" ad (Chapter 2) was used by the Republicans in 1988 against Democratic candidate Governor Michael Dukakis. The ad succeeded in painting Dukakis as weak on fighting crime.

In the 2008 Democratic presidential primaries, Hillary Clinton's "3 a.m. phone call" ad questioned the crisis-management ability of her less-experienced opponent Barack Obama. The ad, which featured a phone ringing in the White House at 3:00 a.m., posed the question of who voters would want to be answering this phone — the experienced Hillary Clinton or the inexperienced Barack Obama.

The "Daisy" and "Willie Horton" ads worked, but Obama defeated Clinton. Democrats mostly wanted change rather than experience.

Negative ads have been used in most democracies, including New Zealand, the United Kingdom, Mexico, and Canada, to name just a few.

Two Canadian negative ads became especially well known. The first was used by the Liberal Party in 1988 to attack Brian Mulroney and the Free Trade Agreement. The ad showed a map of North America and played the voice of an American negotiator saying, "There is just one line we want to change." A hand holding an eraser appeared and wiped out the line between Canada and the United States. Shortly afterward, Liberal support started to increase and Mulroney's Progressive Conservatives soon found themselves in second place.

Pollster Allan Gregg provided Mulroney with some sage advice: "John Turner has established a bridge of trust on free trade between himself and the Canadian people. We need to bomb the bridge." The bridge was bombed by direct Conservative attacks on Turner's credibility, as I have described in Chapter 6, and Mulroney won the election.

The second ad was used in the 1993 federal election by the Progressive Conservatives and was widely seen to be mocking Liberal leader Jean Chrétien's facial deformity. The ensuing public uproar caused the Tories to pull the ad. A sympathetic electorate handed Chrétien a landslide victory.

The small sample of negative ads outlined above seems to support John Sides's hypothesis that negative ads are not as universally successful as conventional wisdom makes them out to be.

My personal experience with negative ads leads me to agree with Professor Sides. It has given me some insights as to what works and what does not. My observations are qualitative and not based upon any quantitative analysis. At the end of this chapter, however, I will review some of the quantitative analyses of the ads used during the 2015 Canadian federal election.

I should first attempt to describe where negative ads fit into the overall advertising continuum. In simple terms, there are three types of ads: (1) positive ads; (2) compare-and-contrast ads; and (3) negative ads. Negative ads can also be divided into three classes, according to my friend John Bowen, the president of Bowen and Binstock: (1) factual from the competitor's standpoint; (2) personal attacks; and (3) out-and-out lies.

"Factual negative" ads are best used as early as possible, Bowen advises that you should define your competition before the competition can define your candidate. Such ads are not personal attacks; rather, they lay out questions that voters should want answered about a competitor so that his or her positions can be compared your candidate's positions.

Personal attack ads are seldom effective and can create sympathy for the candidate being attacked. In extreme cases, they can blow up the attacker's campaign — as in the PCs' 1993 attacks on Chrétien.

Bowen argues that while out-and-out lies can sometimes serve to firm up core supporters, they will do little to attract new supporters.

What are the characteristics of effective ads? What is it about ads that can help, not hurt, a candidate's chance of success?

1990 ONTARIO PROVINCIAL ELECTION

The first negative ads that I used in an election campaign were in the 1990 Ontario election on behalf of Mike Harris and the Ontario PC Party. In Chapter 2, I described the impact of the "Fish Ad," which we released immediately prior to the start of the campaign in an attempt to show that, despite our poor position in the opinion polls, we were ready for a campaign. The other purpose of the ad was to attempt to set the ballot box question that we wanted: Why was Liberal Premier David Peterson calling this early election? We succeeded in getting many voters to continue asking that question right up to election day.

We followed up with negative TV ads during the campaign that also appeared to assist in pushing Peterson out of office on September 5, 1990. John Bowen modestly recalls the impact of the attack ads that he and Eric Bell created for us: "I don't know how many times I was told that our campaign was so good that it put Bob Rae into the premier's office."

Negative ads have to be credible and relevant in order to be effective. There has to be factual information upon which to base the ads. The Peterson government's track record of excessive spending while reducing support for the province's health-care system gave us lots of cover. It also helps if the issue being highlighted by the ads is important to voters. And in 1990, health care and the economy were at the top of voters' concerns.

In my experience, ads that are effective also have to be different and rely heavily on creative imagination. To visually represent the spendthrift ways of the Liberals, one of our television ads showed an exploding piggy bank, while another showed a slowly dripping faucet turn into a gushing torrent of water. A heart monitor screen showing the heartbeat of a living, healthy person going to a dead flat line demonstrated the negative impact of the government's cuts to health care.

While it appeared easy for the Peterson government to spend money it did not have, I recall the difficulty that we had in getting the piggy bank to explode just right. Too much of the explosive was initially used, and the camera was not able to capture the images of the fragments exploding. It took several takes and several piggy banks. Eventually we got it right, and those ads assisted in pulling down the Liberal government.

Peterson's defeat in 1990 was precipitated by his call for an early election, which we were able to tie into the Patti Starr scandal. Patti Starr was a Liberal activist. She was also the CEO of a charity that, under her direction, gave money to the Liberal Party and to Liberal Cabinet ministers. She was charged with election fraud and breach of trust. Her trial was scheduled to start on the day following the provincial election. I had focus groups conducted each week near the end of the campaign as a way of keeping track of any shifts in public opinion. During the last week of the campaign I detected the negative impact of the Starr scandal on Liberal chances. One of the focus group participants claimed to know that Peterson had called the early election for September 6 because Patti Starr was going to trial on September 7. His comment struck a chord with all the other participants.

Each of our ads served to accentuate Peterson's slide during the latter half of the campaign. At the same time, the use of these imaginative negative ads did not appear to hurt us, as we increased our share of the popular vote that we had at the beginning of the campaign.

2000 FEDERAL ELECTION

Now fast forward to 2000 and the federal election campaign for Joe Clark and the Progressive Conservative Party. In Chapter 6, where I discuss the use of research, I described the negative ads produced by Bowen and Binstock that we ran against Jean Chrétien, and the research that was conducted to support the creative content of the ads. Again, the relative success of these ads — we lost the campaign but exceeded expectations and lived to fight another day — can be attributed to the factual evidence that Chrétien had lied and broken a number of promises during his seven years in office. As John Bowen said, "Seeing Chrétien actually saying, 'The GST is gone,' was a good example of factual negative advertising." Bowen and the media-buying company also did a good job in obtaining some unpaid media attention. "The spots were first distributed to the media in advance of their on-air date," Bowen recalls. "Since the TV purchase was necessarily light, targeted but shy of noise level, our buy was leveraged significantly with TV and print coverage of the ads. When the spots aired, many Canadians had already heard of or seen our messaging."

It probably helped that we were a serious underdog during this campaign and were not damaged by our use of the ads; our share of the popular vote increased during the campaign. The success of those ads also demonstrated the value of using humour in a negative ad.

2003 TORONTO MAYORAL ELECTION

David Miller's mayoral campaign in 2003 provided me with another opportunity to use negative ads. In midsummer of that election campaign, Miller was locked in a battle for second place in the race. David and two other candidates trailed badly behind the front-runner, Barbara Hall, who at one point in early 2003 had more than 50 percent of the decided vote, according to polls.

Our campaign then decided to use some of our limited funds to purchase radio spots in order to increase our visibility enough to break out of the pack of second-tier candidates. I met with Geoff Roche, president of Lowe Roche, a Toronto-based agency, to talk about the content of the ads. Geoff, the son of Bob Roche, a legendary North Toronto Tory grassroots organizer, was one of the most creative advertising professionals I have worked with.

I had two instructions for Geoff: make the ads edgy so that they would get noticed, and use either or both of the two issues we felt were important if we were to have any hope of success. These were the planned bridge to the Toronto Island Airport (which David opposed as a means of protecting Toronto's waterfront, as I discuss in Chapter 7) and the elimination of corruption at city hall (David had been a leader in uncovering a computer-leasing scandal during his time as a Metro Toronto councillor).

The agency came back with two radio spots. The first addressed the quality of life on Toronto's waterfront. In the ad, a soft-spoken man describes the tranquillity and beauty of the waterfront; his voice was then drowned out by the increasing roar of aircraft engines. The ad later received an "okay" reaction from political observers.

But the second ad was a home run. It was a negative ad directed at my own candidate. The ad featured a gruff, sleazy-sounding lobbyist who was urging voters not to vote for David Miller. Miller, he declared, would strengthen the rules governing lobbying at city hall, and this would damage his livelihood, cut into his ability to send his kids to private school, and upset his plans to continue to vacation in the Cayman Islands, a well-known haven for tax avoidance. To my knowledge, this was the only time a negative ad had been used by a campaign against its own candidate. The ad was seen as imaginative and humorous.

Before we aired the ads I took them to my campaign executive committee for their reactions. In retrospect, I probably should not have done that. In my experience it is almost impossible to test negative ads, and this group of dedicated Miller supporters was no different. People will tell you usually that they do not like negative and prefer positive messages. What they cannot tell you is if the negative ads will work for your candidate.

Members of my executive committee liked the waterfront ad but were really nervous about the lobbyist ad and feared it might backfire on the campaign. After some time I brought the discussion to an end. I said we really did need to get noticed, and I understood that there could be a backlash. Then I put this question to them:"What are we afraid of? We could go from 3 percent to 1 percent in the polls?"

We ran both ads, but the lobbyist ad was run twice as often as the waterfront ad. Fortunately, our poll numbers began to rise, partly due to our radio spots. Voters started to notice David.

The agency was over-the-moon excited with the reaction to the "Don't vote for David Miller" lobbyist ad, and two weeks later Geoff called to tell me that they had a concept they wanted to show me for the next phase of our advertising campaign. It was a full-blown campaign based on the theme "Don't vote for David Miller!" with buttons, posters, and radio and TV scripts.

I politely said no — once was enough. We needed to move on to other issues that would positively market David now that we had voters' attention.

Over the next few months we created an imaginative and cheeky set of posters using an image of David in a stand-up position with a variety of phrases.

- Looks like a Mayor — Thinks like a Mayor — Talks like a Neighbour
- Backroom Boys Start Packing!
- He has the answers. And they're not on a teleprompter!
- Extraordinary Vision! Extraordinary Leadership! Extraordinary Hair!

We also needed to continue our fight against the bridge to the Island Airport, which had become a unique policy position for our campaign. The other major candidates all supported building the bridge because they claimed it would be a boost to downtown businesses. We decided to

Being edgy. Getting noticed. One of a series of six posters used in David Miller's Toronto mayoral campaign, 2003.

EXTRAORDINARY VISION.
EXTRAORDINARY LEADERSHIP.
EXTRAORDINARY HAIR.

david miller mayor
FOR A CLEAN CITY

THE ISLAND AIRPORT EXPANSION.
IT'LL BE LIKE THE AIR SHOW.
ONLY 365 DAYS A YEAR.

THE ISLAND AIRPORT AFFECTS OUR FUTURE. A FUTURE ONLY
one candidate is thinking about. David Miller knows there is a lot at stake
in the race for our next mayor. And it's not just the waterfront. It's the future of this city. Ultimately, the city we leave
our children. We can't explain why Ms. Hall and Mr. Tory support the Island Airport expansion. We can, however,
explain how David Miller, because of his views on this issue and many others, plans to make our city great again.

WATERFRONT CONCERTS: NOW WITH | WHO'S FOR DESTROYING | EVEN THE TORONTO CANCER
DOZENS OF INTERMISSIONS. | OUR WATERFRONT? | PREVENTION COALITION IS AGAINST IT.

DAVID MILLER. WHY HE'S THE RIGHT GUY FOR THE JOB.

A picture is always worth a thousand words. Ad/pamphlet used in David Miller's Toronto mayoralty campaign showing the negative impact of building a bridge to the Toronto Island Billy Bishop Airport.

use negative ads not against other candidates, but against the bridge. My favourite was a print ad that showed thirty airplanes flying in tight formation over the peaceful and tranquil Toronto Islands and waterfront.

I realized how effective that ad was at the end of the campaign when I was on the receiving end of a telephone call from a representative of Porter Airlines, the major tenant at the Island Airport, blasting me for exaggerating the number of aircraft that would be using the airport at any one time. I could not disagree and merely used literary licence as my excuse.

David Miller was elected on November 10, 2003, becoming the sixty-third mayor of Toronto. The negative ads were a small, but important, part of his success.

2014 TORONTO MAYORAL ELECTION

My most recent direct experience with the use of negative ads was during the 2014 Toronto mayoral race as campaign director for Olivia Chow (I have examined this campaign from many different angles in earlier chapters.) Olivia started the race that January as the front-runner in all the polls, and she kept her lead until July 2014. Two major events occurred in mid-summer that disrupted the campaign. The Liberals under Kathleen Wynne won the Ontario provincial election on June 12, 2014; and on April 30, the then mayor of Toronto, Rob Ford, checked himself into rehab and suspended his campaign. On June 30, Ford returned from his stint in rehab and resumed his campaign.

We decided that we needed a pivot point to start the next phase of the campaign, leading up to Labour Day. We decided to hold a rally and volunteer-training session in downtown Toronto and to release a radio ad welcoming Rob Ford back into the campaign. The ad was to use humour. What could go wrong?

We produced the ad, which had three different individuals welcoming Ford back to the campaign with very short comments that were meant to be funny. I recall one of the women in the ad saying that she would have to cover up her young daughter's ears so that she wouldn't hear any of Ford's famous bombastic comments.

As described in Chapter 2 where I discuss managing expectations, Olivia's lead in the polls disappeared during nine days in early July. Our strength with female voters in downtown Toronto had been neutralized by Tory. I listened to the progressive women from downtown Toronto in the mid-July focus group after our vote had collapsed. While they did not mention the radio ad specifically, they expressed a concern that Olivia was being excessively nasty to Mayor Ford. Three months earlier these same women had been appalled by the vulgar and embarrassing antics of Rob Ford. Now they were saying that anyone returning from rehab deserves a second chance! The radio commercial was the only activity in our campaign during early July, so we knew our attempt at humour had backfired.

That ad was not the last of the negative ads seen in the mayoral campaign. Doug Ford, Rob's older brother, replaced Rob on the ballot in early September after it was announced that Rob had a serious form of cancer and would be undergoing treatment. The Ford campaign then relied heavily on an air game, as they had little time to put a ground game or organization in place. They developed a series of radio and TV ads attacking John Tory for various inconsistencies. They were all done with the mocking theme line, "What's the Story, Mr. Tory?"

Jeff Silverstein, communications director for the Doug Ford mayoral campaign, believes that their ads worked and helped to helped to turn their campaign around. "These ads were not negative ads, really. All we were saying is take a second look at Tory. There are some things missing from his resumé, and he has changed his positions on a number of issues. The ads worked, but we ran out of money to air these ads with enough weight to close the deal."

Despite those ads, John Tory won the election on October 27 with a significant lead over Doug Ford. The voters had decided that only Tory could defeat the Fords, and no amount of negative advertising would reduce their desire for change.

2008, 2011, AND 2015 FEDERAL ELECTIONS

The use of negative ads in the last three Canadian federal elections (2008, 2011, and 2015) also deserves comment here.

Stephen Harper and his Conservative Party won a minority government in 2006, defeating Prime Minister Paul Martin's Liberal Party. Shortly after, Martin stepped down as leader.

The Liberals then changed leaders three times between 2006 and 2013.

Stéphane Dion was the surprise winner of the Liberal leadership in 2007, and before the convention was even over Harper's Conservatives launched a set of negative ads portraying Dion as a weak and indecisive leader. Dion never recovered, and in the October 2008 election the Liberals won just seventy-seven seats in the House of Commons.

Shortly after, Dion stepped down as leader.

Michael Ignatieff had been persuaded to return from his professorship at Harvard to run for the leadership in 2007, but he had lost to Dion at that convention. He subsequently won a seat in the House of Commons in the 2008 campaign. After Dion resigned, he announced he would run again for the leadership, which he won at the convention on December 10, 2008.

The Conservative attack ads started immediately, using several different lines. The most effective one seemed to me to be the "Just Visiting" attack ad, which positioned Ignatieff as an opportunist and an elitist who had come back from abroad only to become prime minister. The ad worked, and combined with a weak Liberal campaign and a surprisingly strong campaign by Jack Layton and the NDP, it led to the Liberals being crushed. They were reduced to just thirty-four seats in the May 2011 election, an all-time low.

Shortly after, Ignatieff stepped down as leader.

The Liberals scheduled another leadership convention, and in April 2013, Justin Trudeau, the son of former prime minister Pierre Trudeau, became the leader of the Liberal Party of Canada.

The Conservatives were ready for him. They created the now somewhat infamous ad that showed an interviewing committee assessing the resumé of Trudeau's limited experience when applying for the job of prime minister. The ad concluded with a light touch of humour, with one older, somewhat balding interviewer saying, "Nice hair, though." The tagline for the ad was "Just Not Ready."

Some of us believe that these particular ads against Justin Trudeau were personally important for Stephen Harper. Harper vehemently opposed everything that Justin's father had stood for in government — social programs, a larger role for government, and increased deficits to make investments in the economy. In October 2000, two days after Pierre Trudeau's funeral, Harper had written a bitter critique of the former prime minister's policy record.

The Conservatives spent a lot of money on airing the "Just Not Ready" ad in the three months leading up to the 2015 federal election. One piece of quantitative research assessing the effectiveness of this and other campaign ads reported that 72 percent of Canadians claimed to have seen the commercial. This is an astoundingly high level of recognition for any kind of ad. The highest recall for all of the other ads that were tested at the same time for the three major parties was in the low 20 percent range. A quantitative assessment of the ad conducted by Innovative Research showed that the ad was very effective in pulling down the Liberal vote during the pre-writ period.

These ads helped to create very low expectations for Trudeau as he headed into the 2015 campaign (as I discuss in Chapter 2). He used these low expectations to his advantage and was generally seen by most to have been the winner of the first two televised campaign debates. He was assisted by the Conservative campaign spokesperson, Kory Teneycke, who surprisingly (and carelessly) told the media, just before the first debate, that Trudeau "would win debate points if he comes on stage with his pants on."

As a market researcher I have always believed that quantitative and qualitative research cannot be used to evaluate the effectiveness of negative ads. I have tried, but the usual response from voters is, "Why don't they tell me something positive about their candidate?"

Even when pushed in focus groups or personal interviews, respondents are not likely to admit that their vote would be swayed by a negative ad. And yet evidence exists that negative ads do work — sometimes.

During the 2015 campaign I was interested to note that an old friend of mine, Greg Lyle, the president of Innovative Research, had been commissioned by the *Globe and Mail* to conduct quantitative research to evaluate the ads used by all the three major political parties in the pre-writ and writ periods of the election.

The Liberals used imagination and conviction in producing an ad that was a direct rebuttal to the Conservative ad that claimed Trudeau was just not ready. Conventional political wisdom is that you should never repeat a negative attack against yourself. Trudeau and the Liberals took a chance and used the attack line before pivoting to his positive line: "Some people say that I am not ready. I will tell you what I am not ready for, and that is to watch hard-working Canadians lose jobs and fall further behind, and I am ready instead to raise taxes on the rich." Greg Lyle reported that this ad worked very well for the Liberals.

The most surprising results for me came from Lyle's assessment of the Conservative ads. He tested both their negative and positive ads. The negative ads against the Liberals had little or no impact upon respondents' intention to vote Liberal or NDP. However, the intention to vote Conservative was significantly reduced by exposure to these ads. Even more surprising was the negative reaction during the campaign to the "Just Not Ready" ad that had been so effective in pulling Trudeau and the Liberals down in the pre-writ period. When assessed during the election period, it only had a slight negative impact on the Liberals but significantly decreased the Conservatives' voter intention numbers.

The positive Conservative ads had little or no impact upon respondents' intentions to vote Liberal or NDP, but, surprisingly, they slightly reduced their intention to vote Conservative. Lyle's studies indicated the Conservatives were apparently between a rock and a hard place. They had called an early, very long election, supposedly because of the increased spending limits that only they, with their large war chest, could take advantage of. They then discovered that both their positive and negative ads were driving down voters' intention to vote for Harper and his party.

My conclusions regarding these Conservative test results are that the high level of acceptance for the time-for-a-change call may have drowned out the messages the Tories were trying to present, and that voters had grown weary of the "Just Not Ready" pitch. Because they had seen so much of the ad in the pre-writ period, it lost its impact.

I believe that negative political ads, like any other weapon in the campaign manager's arsenal, do not win or lose elections. Candidates do. In the vast majority of cases, candidates win or lose on their merits — I believe that. After all, their names are on the ballot. Negative ads, tour strategy, organization strategy, and policy platform are important, but they are all supporting elements for the main actors on the stage — the candidates.

I have become a believer in John Sides's hypothesis that negative ads work, except when they do not work. As Jeff Silverstein says, "They can be effective, but can equally backfire. It is a tough thing to get right. It's like playing with fire."

It seems to me that use of humour, imagination, and thinking outside the box can help make negative ads effective. Attack ads need to be credible and not too over the top. It helps if your candidate is an underdog or challenger and not an incumbent preaching from a bully pulpit, because, after all, Canadians place a high value on fairness and will generally give an underdog more leeway and support.

Negative ads, and the staff required to execute a social-media campaign and to operate a war room, all require money. They contribute to the high cost of running a campaign. The next chapter will deal with the role and influence of money in the political process.

Chapter 11

The Influence of Money in Politics

Anyone running for leadership should put their credit cards under a pound of pork in the freezer and don't tell anyone where they are.

— HUGH SEGAL

My old friend Hugh Segal knows whereof he speaks. The Progressive Conservative Party was on its last legs in 1998 when Segal — later a senator and currently the master of Massey College at the University of Toronto — decided to contest its leadership. The party had been devastated in the 1993 election, reduced to just two seats in Parliament as the Liberals under Jean Chrétien stormed to a majority government. By 1998 the PCs were so broke that they could not afford to hold a traditional convention to choose a new leader to replace Jean Charest, who had left federal politics to become the Liberal leader in Quebec.

Even so, five brave (or foolhardy) souls decided to seek the leadership. Segal, who had served as chief of staff to both Prime Minister Brian Mulroney and Ontario Premier William Davis, was one of them. Not only did Segal not win — he finished second to Joe Clark, who had come out of political retirement for a second go-around as leader — the cost of his campaign nearly wiped out Segal and his wife financially. As Segal ruefully acknowledged, he should have taken his own advice and buried his credit cards in the freezer:

> Towards the end of the leadership I was convinced by members of my campaign team that I should fly out

to Saskatchewan to meet with a number of party delegates. Six people showed up at the meeting. It was quite discouraging. As I returned to my hotel room, the telephone rang. It was my wife, Donna. She started the conversation with "Hugh, your Diner's Club statement came in the mail today. Are you using your card for the campaign? Hugh, the balance is $90,000!" I explained to Donna that the campaign was going through a bit of a dry spell in its fundraising and that they had asked me to provide the card to see us through this period.

The "bit of a dry spell" did not end there for the Progressive Conservatives. Five years later, in 2003, the party merged with — or, perhaps more correctly, was absorbed by — the right-wing Canadian Alliance, and out of that union came the new Conservative Party under the leadership of Stephen Harper.

Money can be the elephant in the room for parties and candidates alike. If finances are not handled skillfully and firmly from the outset in a campaign, they can upset all the best-laid plans and doom the campaign to failure.

The role of a campaign manager is to look after the candidate in all aspects of the campaign. There can be no daylight between the candidate and the campaign manager on any issue, whether it be policy, organization, strategic plan, performance of the candidate, or finances. With respect to finances, it is the responsibility of the campaign manager to keep pressure on the fundraisers to meet the campaign's financial targets. In addition, the candidate and his or her campaign manager need to have an exact understanding of the degree of risk that the candidate is prepared to assume and, if things do not go the way they both hope, what level of debt the candidate is prepared to accept at the end of the campaign.

I have come to a variety of understandings with candidates over the years. In 2004, John Tory and I agreed the campaign debt would not exceed $100,000 for his Ontario PC Party leadership bid. Olivia Chow agreed to a similar financial commitment for her mayoral campaign in Toronto in 2014.

In 2003, I was asked to manage Peter MacKay's campaign for the leadership of the national Progressive Conservative Party some two months after his campaign had started. On my first day in the office I asked to see the books. I wanted to know how much had been raised and what the budgets were.

As I recall, the operating budget was approximately $2 million, of which just $200,000 had been raised. I sat down with Bob Plamondon, Peter's financial agent, that afternoon and we cut the budget to $1 million. This is one of the first principles of fundraising: a dollar saved equals a dollar raised.

I then dealt with Peter and his father, Elmer MacKay, and we agreed that the debt at the end would be a maximum of $100,000. Peter went on to win the leadership and I kept my commitment to the two MacKays.

I cannot report that all of my campaigns have worked out as well financially. In 1983 the John Crosbie leadership campaign was one such example. Our campaign caught fire near the end, and although we had tight financial controls, I learned after the campaign that they were not able to withstand the enthusiasm of all the people who showed up in Ottawa to help John. When the dust cleared the campaign was $750,000 short.

I learned from Frank Ryan and Basil Dobbin, the two fundraising co-chairs from St. John's, how to deal with a shortfall. They froze all payments and waited until all the invoices were received. The invoices dribbled in over the next two months. (That is another reality of campaign financing: invoices will continue to arrive at campaign headquarters long after it seems reasonable, and few if any of the campaign staff will recall ordering the service, the coffee, or the materials on the invoice.) Frank and Basil went to work negotiating with each of the creditors. Their approach was simple: "You will be paid, but it may take a long time. We have plans to raise funds, but that will take time. However, if you can reduce your bill, we have some cash and you could get paid sooner."

Over one-half of the debt was negotiated away. A large fundraiser in Toronto took care of the next chunk, and a lot of hard work raised the rest. This included going back to our original donors, who had been very generous, and asking them for a little bit more. Another fundraising lesson — a giver is a giver is a giver.

I learned another lesson on that campaign — 50 percent of the funds required for a campaign should come from the candidate's home base of political support. That applied in Crosbie's leadership campaign, where half of the money came from Newfoundland, and in Mike Harris's 1990 PC leadership bid in Ontario, where 50 percent came from North Bay. These were not wealthy places at the time, but the pride that comes from communities thinking that their local man or woman might be a provincial or national figure can be leveraged to raise substantial amounts of cash.

However, there can be a point in a campaign when it becomes obvious that unless significant changes are made to spending plans, there will be a shortfall, and at that point the campaign manager owes it to the candidate to have a conversation about next steps. Stay in the race? Get out? Cut the spending? Find some bridge financing?

I have seen a number of situations where an under-abundance of funding has turned out to be a blessing or a cloud with a silver lining. When funds are scarce, the principle that necessity is the mother of invention comes into play. Wiser choices get made by campaign managers.

I remember that in the 1990 Mike Harris leadership race we believed we needed to distribute a comprehensive policy brochure to all party members (some 34,000 individuals). We did not have a lot to spend on this. I had a conversation with a supporter who ran a printing company. I told him that I needed to print this document on the cheap. His company had a fast-food client for whom they regularly printed placemats used on the trays to carry food to the tables. As I described my needs, he picked up a sheet of paper and folded it so that it would have sixteen panels. He asked if I could put all of the policy content into this format. They were printed for pennies each, and we were able to distribute the platform to each party member. As I recall, the supporter also paid for the printing.

Candidates may at some point need to decide whether the campaign should, or should not, continue. It takes courage to put a second mortgage on a home or arrange an overdraft at the bank, but as long as candidates believe they can manage the shortfall after the election, then

One of the first successful examples of customer relationship management. This photo of Brian Mulroney and his family was sent out to all PC Canada Fund donors at the end of 1983. There was no direct request for donations, yet over $40,000 poured in.

they should continue to fight to the end. They cannot win if their names are not on the ballot.

If they lose, they will need to use the lessons from Frank Ryan and Basil Dobbin from Newfoundland to work down the debt. If they win, I would simply observe that money loves power; any deficit will be taken care of.

Rob Ford's winning campaign for the 2010 Toronto mayoral election provides a prime example of the latter point. Rob and his brother Doug are both millionaires and, as a subsequent financial audit revealed, the campaign that year was bankrolled by their family business. The campaign ran up just over $1.3 million in expenditures; that came under the legal spending limit, but when the victory party and fundraising costs were added, their outstanding debt was some $750,000.

Not to fear, along came the "money loves power" donors. John Tory, the current mayor of Toronto, and some of the traditional municipal fundraisers and former provincial premiers stepped up and put on a fundraiser to eliminate the debts of all of the candidates. My candidate,

Joe Pantalone, was the only one to refuse this assistance. While each of the other losing candidates received some help, by far the bulk of the money raised — some $750,000 — went to paying off Mayor Ford's debt.

This was just one example of money coming to support power. Our 2003 David Miller mayoral campaign finished with a relatively modest $175,000 shortfall on election night. David had defeated John Tory. Tory took the lead and graciously offered to attend a fundraising event for Miller to erase the debt.

In 2015 I observed that Patrick Brown had spent some $2 million to win the leadership of the PC Party of Ontario. At the time of writing this book, he had a personal debt of $375,000. Time will tell whether money still likes power or potential power.

I am not against the practice of financially supporting the winner after the fact, provided that it is clear that the donors are not buying access or favours and that there is full disclosure of the donors and size of donations. I know that the Miller administration was not influenced by any political donations, regardless of when they were received. David introduced a number of processes and offices to produce an open and accountable city government, including a lobbyist registration system and an Office of the Integrity Commissioner.

While money does flow to power and, to a certain extent, to potential power, I believe that the candidate who spends the most money will not necessarily win. In a very real sense money is just like any other tool in a campaign manager's tool kit: its role is to support the main actor on the political stage. That is the candidate.

Consider the examples of the last four Toronto mayoral contests.

In 2003 John Tory outspent David Miller. Miller won.

In 2006 David Miller outspent Jane Pitfield. Miller won.

In 2010 George Smitherman outspent Rob Ford. Ford won.

In 2014 John Tory spent approximately the same amount as Rob and Doug Ford combined. Tory won.

Money does not appear to have been a deciding factor in the above successes.

When Geoff Stevens and I wrote *Leaders and Lesser Mortals* in 1992, we feared that leadership contests at that time were being unduly influenced by money. The one notable exception was the 1976 PC Party of Canada leadership, which was won by Joe Clark even though five other candidates each spent considerably more than Clark. Since the 1980s, political parties, at both the federal and provincial levels, have been introducing spending limits for leadership campaigns, and they seem to have altered the financial landscape.

An examination of recent leadership campaigns in Canada suggests that here, too, spending the most money does not always translate into success.

I have tried to gather, as best I could, the financial records of the most recent leadership campaigns at the federal level and for the four largest provinces in Canada (Ontario, Quebec, British Columbia, and Alberta). While I have been unable to find all of these records starting in 2000, I have been able to access the majority of them.

During this period, the following leadership contestants spent the most money and won their respective leadership campaigns:

- Peter MacKay — 2003, PC Party of Canada
- Jack Layton — 2004, federal NDP
- Elizabeth May — 2006, federal Green Party (spent just $9,000 more than her closest opponent)
- Michael Ignatieff — 2008, Liberal Party of Canada
- Tim Hudak — 2009, Ontario PC Party
- Thomas Mulcair — 2012, federal NDP (spent just 8 percent more than Brian Topp, the second-place competitor)
- Jim Prentice — 2013, Alberta PC party
- Philippe Couillard — 2013, Quebec Liberal Party
- Justin Trudeau — 2013, Liberal Party of Canada
- Patrick Brown — 2015, Ontario PC Party

During this same period, the following contestants won their leadership campaigns despite being outspent by one or more of their competitors:

- Stephen Harper — 2004, Conservative Party of Canada
- Stéphane Dion — 2006, Liberal Party of Canada
- Christy Clark — 2011, British Columbia Liberal Party
- Andrea Horwath — 2012, Ontario NDP
- Kathleen Wynne — 2013, Ontario Liberal Party
- Rachel Notley — 2013, Alberta NDP

While the sample size of the above leadership campaigns is small, it is apparent that spending more money does not guarantee electoral success.

Finally, a review of the spending of the last two federal elections suggests that money does not buy or even rent elections.

In 2011 the three major parties (Conservatives, Liberals, NDP) each spent approximately $20 million, just under the allowable spending limit of $21 million. In fact, during that election the second-place NDP reported spending $800,000 more than the Conservatives, who won a majority government.

In 2015 the combination of new additional constituencies and an extra-long campaign raised the per-party spending ceiling to $54.9 million. The Liberals, who won a majority government, spent $43.1 million, slightly more than the Conservatives, at $41.9 million. (That both parties spent far less than the allowable limit suggests they each had difficulty raising or borrowing money.)

The results reported in this chapter suggest that money plays a supporting role in determining electoral success, similar to the roles played by policy, war rooms, negative ads, organization, and all of the other tools in the campaign manager's tool kit. Some of the legislative changes made over the last forty-plus years, disclosure of larger donations, campaign spending limits, and limits on the size of donations, seem to have helped protect Canadian politics from the excesses that have infiltrated American politics, where it takes over $1 billion to win the White House and where Super PACs (political action committees) spend an additional 65 to 70 percent beyond that total.

The process of legislative changes to elections and fundraising laws appears likely to continue in Canada. Recently, three issues have attracted significant media and public attention, particularly in Ontario and British Columbia: unlimited third-party advertising; the practice of parties in government appearing to be selling access to premiers and Cabinet ministers to donors who write big cheques; and the question of whether unions and corporations should continue to be allowed to make political contributions.

Andrew Hodgson, an old friend of mine from Haliburton, Ontario, and one of the best grassroots organizers that I have worked with, believes that third-party advertising is one of the most serious issues facing elective politics in Canada today. I tend to agree, especially when one observes that third-party groups spent almost $9 million in the 2014 Ontario provincial election, while each of the parties had a limit of approximately $7.5 million.

Time will tell what further changes will be introduced. I would support a cap on third-party advertising during elections similar to the federal laws, but I would oppose any move to ban unions and corporations from making political donations. After all, each of these entities is part of our society and is affected by the actions of government. Why should they not be allowed to participate, as long as there are caps on the size of donations and speedy disclosure of all donations?

As Geoff and I concluded in *Leaders and Lesser Mortals* back in 1992: "Money is important in politics in Canada. It buys the polling and the television time. It is the grease that keeps the machine running smoothly. But it is not the only thing that makes the political world go round. That is as it should be in a democracy."

We have discussed the importance of having a well-prepared candidate, a relevant campaign platform, a war room and communications team in place, and adequate funding. One would assume that with all of these taken care of, all the crucial aspects of a campaign would be in place. With all of those details looked after, one could ask, "What could go wrong?"

The answer in politics is: everything.

Murphy's law — "Anything that can go wrong will go wrong" — was made for politics. Unforeseen events will invariably happen.

In my experience good candidates and good campaign personnel will usually be able to deal with the unexpected. What campaigns are usually not able to deal with is friendly fire — that is, comments or actions from their own team members who have decided that their personal interests are more important than the good of the team.

I will use the next chapter to describe two campaigns that I was involved with where undisciplined members of our team chose to jump ship in mid-campaign in attempts to save their own skins, regardless of the consequences for the rest of the team.

Chapter 12

The Importance of Party Discipline

Thou shalt not speak ill of any fellow Republican.
— RONALD REAGAN

Ronald Reagan's admonition was not just good manners but also great politics. As pollsters attest, voters are repelled by divided parties. When politicians are focused on fighting each other rather than their opponents, the result is invariably defeat.

Stephen Harper was a leader who understood this. In his years as leader of the Conservative Party and as prime minister, he developed a reputation of being a control freak. He was obsessive in his insistence on discipline on the part of his Cabinet, his caucus, and his Conservative Party organization. Everyone was expected to stay on message, as laid down by the leader, to recite the prescribed "talking points," and to observe the "media lines" approved by Harper and his office. In the 2015 federal election, this all-control-all-the-time approach to campaigning extended to ordering local Conservative candidates not to speak to the media or even to take part in all-candidates meetings.

Part of this insistence on discipline stemmed from Harper's own controlling personality, but part of it was a product of the problems the Tories had had in the past with loose cannons, candidates who thought it was perfectly fine to chart their own way and to observe party direction when it suited them and to ignore it when it did not.

* * *

As national director of the Progressive Conservative Party of Canada in the early 1970s, I came to understand first-hand the importance of discipline in party politics and the influence that lack of discipline had upon voters.

Robert Lorne Stanfield was the national leader of the party at that time. He had lost resoundingly to Pierre Trudeau in 1968, but had come within two seats of defeating Trudeau in the fall of 1972. Trudeau's large electoral advantage came from Quebec and the francophone seats in New Brunswick. In most federal elections at the time, the Liberals would be ahead by some seventy-five seats by the time the vote counting reached Ontario, making it very difficult for the Tories to win. During that time the Conservatives had, for a number of reasons, also gained the reputation of being anti-French, not the least of which was their checkered record with respect to supporting official bilingualism for federal government services.

Opposition to official bilingualism came from a number of Conservative MPs in rural Ontario and many from Alberta, Saskatchewan, and Manitoba. Regardless of the Conservative Party's opposition, the Official Languages Act was passed in 1969. This legislation gave English and French equal status in the government of Canada.

Even though the legislation was in place, the Liberal government in the early 1970s introduced a motion into the House of Commons asking MPs to reconfirm their support for the concept of official bilingualism. They did this knowing full well that the Tory caucus would split ranks and thereby reinforce its image of being divided and anti-French. Stanfield spent countless hours trying to manage the split, but there were a baker's dozen of MPs who insisted on voting their conscience. They were not at all interested in demonstrating that the party was united and ready to form a government. I had the feeling that whenever the party started to get some traction against the Liberals, Trudeau's Liberals would throw a motion like this on to the legislative agenda — like a piece of red meat into a pool of sharks — to watch the Conservatives destroy themselves.

The Liberals also devised other ways to show that the Conservatives were not united and thus not worthy of being considered competent to govern.

I recall that just before Christmas in both 1972 and 1973, the Liberals introduced motions calling for raises for members of Parliament. They would then watch a number of Tory MPs stand up and vote against these motions. Stanfield, a multi-millionaire who did not need the extra cash, would entreat members of his caucus to vote in support of increased pay for MPs. He was basically saying that in order to attract better people to elected public service you have to make the remuneration attractive. He never put it this way, but in essence what he was saying was, if you pay peanuts, you get monkeys! Regardless, there were always some "principled" MPs who played into the Liberals' hands by voting against a pay raise.

Stanfield's political career ended in 1974 when he lost to Trudeau and the Liberals in the "wage and price controls election" that I describe briefly in Chapter 7. The PCs had entered that election with a reasonable chance of winning. Inflation and mortgages rates were close to 11 percent and rising. People were hurting. The Conservative platform proposed a ninety-day wage and price freeze to shock-stop the rise in inflation.

Pierre Trudeau and the Liberals were having none of it. Trudeau came up with a very effective communications line to counter our policy. "Zap! You're frozen!" became his signature line.

While the line was effective, the real damage to Stanfield and the Tories was inflicted by a lack of discipline on the part of key members of the Conservatives' own team.

Party policy had been developed during 1973 and early 1974 by a policy coordinating committee of the party that reported to Stanfield. It was chaired by Tom Symons, founding president of Trent University in Peterborough. Jim Gillies, MP for Don Valley West in Toronto, was the caucus representative on that committee. He was an academic and an economist who had been chair of the Ontario Economic Council in 1971 and 1972.

Gillies was instrumental in developing the wage and price control policy. I sat at the policy table as it was being developed. The committee was persuaded by Gillies that a freeze followed by controls was the right prescription for Canada in those troubling times. However, partway through the election, Gillies began to hear rumbles of unrest from Don Valley West. Worried about his seat, he equivocated on the policy that he had been instrumental in getting the party to adopt. The result was big news in the media, and it sent a chill through the Tory campaign.

The second prominent Conservative candidate to disagree with the party policy was former prime minister John Diefenbaker. The Stanfield team had been worried about what "the Chief" might say during the campaign. As everyone knew, he had been voted out of the leadership in 1966–67. And as everyone also knew, Dief had neither forgotten nor forgiven. The campaign team arranged for Bill Liaskas, a veteran political operative from London, Ontario, to travel with Diefenbaker during the campaign as sort of a babysitter/manager. We hoped that Liaskas would be able to keep the former PM on message. He had a reasonably good relationship with Diefenbaker, and we thought we might be able to get through the campaign without trouble from that direction.

Fat chance!

Ten days before the election, Diefenbaker was in Prince Edward Island where he spoke in support of one-half of the party policy. He said he was in favour of price controls but not wage controls. Once again, Tory disunity was on full public display. More evidence for the voters that the PC Party was not united. The media had a field day.

On July 10, Pierre Trudeau and the Liberals were elected with a majority government, due in no small part to the Conservatives' lack of party discipline. The day the Conservatives lost the 1974 election, Jim Gillies, who had tried to disown his own policy, also went down to defeat.

But politics is a fickle and cynical game. Fifteen months later, at Thanksgiving season in October 1975, Trudeau summoned the provincial premiers to Ottawa. There he announced the introduction of his own pro-gram to control prices and wages and the establishment of the Anti-Inflation Board to manage the controls process. For Trudeau, the result of his flip-flop was short-term gain for longer-term pain. He was defeated by Joe Clark, Stanfield's successor, in 1979. He later admitted that his reversal on wage and price controls contributed much to his defeat that year.

Three decades later, I found myself directing the 2007 Ontario provincial campaign for John Tory and the Ontario PCs, and I observed once again the devastating impact that lack of party discipline can have on electoral success. (Chapters 6 and 8 also discuss this election, from the perspectives of researching public reaction to campaign ads, and of headquarters organization, respectively.)

It is conventional wisdom that Tory lost the 2007 election to Dalton McGuinty mainly because of the Conservatives' new policy of support for public funding for faith-based schools. Not entirely! There were a number of factors at play, but in my opinion, backed up by our nightly tracking research, none was more important than the lack of discipline in our team.

An analysis of the party research conducted prior to and during the 2007 election campaign revealed a number of shortcomings. We went into the campaign facing various challenges. These included a relatively low level of desire for change amongst the electorate; a lower level of support from females, visible minorities, and residents of urban Ontario; and a low level of second-choice support from voters intending to cast their ballots for the NDP or the Green Party. However, a major factor in our 2007 defeat was the lack of discipline during the last ten days of the campaign exhibited by two of our candidates who were both sitting MPPs.

First, the faith-based funding issue. Ontario was, and continues to be, the only province in Canada that fully funds a Catholic education while not providing funding to other religious schools. Catholic funding was guaranteed at the elementary level through the British North America Act passed in 1867, and funding was later extended to the secondary school level. Over the years there have been a number of court challenges brought forward by faith-based schools. In 1999 the United Nations Human Rights Committee determined that the Ontario funding system was discriminatory.

In 2003 then-Premier Ernie Eves and his treasurer, Jim Flaherty, introduced a $500 tax credit for any taxpayer who had a child attending a religious or independent school in Ontario. When Eves was defeated in 2003 by Liberal Dalton McGuinty, the tax credit was retroactively cancelled.

During the 2004 Ontario Progressive Conservative leadership race to select a successor to Eves, John Tory, Frank Klees, and Jim Flaherty were the major contenders. Each of these candidates had a policy position on faith-based education. Each of them was vague about how he would address this issue, but address it each would, if elected leader.

During the leadership campaign I told Tory that this vague promise could prove problematic in the next provincial election. Regardless, he included the policy in his leadership platform. Tory won the leadership on the second ballot, defeating Flaherty.

As campaign director for the party in the election that followed, I had a number of early challenges, not the least of which was to ensure that Tory could win a seat in the Ontario Legislature. That took some time, but in March 2005 he won a by-election in Ernie Eves's old seat of Dufferin-Peel-Wellington-Grey (renamed Dufferin-Caledon in 2007). However, the principal challenge was to find a faith-based education policy position that we could include in the party's election platform.

We asked John Matheson, a partner in a Toronto-based government relations firm, StrategyCorp, to head our policy/platform committee. Matheson assembled a team with representation from diverse segments of the party, including the caucus, and they consulted widely. Positions on the two most important issues for all Ontarians — economy and health care — turned out to be relatively easy to develop.

Dealing with faith-based funding was not so easy.

In early 2007 I asked Tory if we could run our campaign saying only that a Conservative government would deal with this issue once it had been elected. He said no. He had made a promise to party members during the leadership, and he intended to honour it. He said he believed that politicians should keep their word — something that Liberal Premier Dalton McGuinty was not known for. (In the 2003 election McGuinty had promised not to raise taxes. Four weeks after his election, he introduced a new health-care premium — a tax by any other name.) Tory was convinced that Ontarians would vote for a straight-talking leader, and he was anxious to present himself in that light.

When the issue heated up in early September of the 2007 campaign, Tory explained his rationale: it was a policy based on fairness and a determination to build a more inclusive public education system. "I am actually being honest with people and taking a principled stand which is tough to do but right," he said, adding, "If I changed course now and said I had made an error —which I do not believe I have — that would either indicate weak leadership in not thinking something through or weak leadership which flip-flops at the first sign of trouble."

Not only was Tory's pledge regarding faith-based school funding going to cause him trouble, but a second promise that he made during the leadership also came back to bite him in the election. He had been impressed by Brian Mulroney's courage in the 1984 federal election in leaving a safe seat in Nova Scotia to run in his home province in Quebec, where PC candidates rarely won. Tory was also determined to run in a riding where he lived, that is, in Toronto.

However, in the years after Bill Davis's premiership, the Conservatives had had great trouble winning provincial seats in the large urban centres of Ontario: Toronto, Ottawa, Hamilton, and London. In fact, by 2007 the party did not hold a single seat in any of those cities. Nevertheless, during his 2004 leadership bid, Tory followed Mulroney's example and pledged to run in a Toronto riding. He was convinced the party could not win the province until it could win in the capital.

Tory could have stayed in rural Dufferin-Caledon and been re-elected without breaking a sweat, but in his mind that was not an option. He chose the Toronto riding of Don Valley West, where he and his family had lived for almost fifty years.

Many questioned his judgment on both his riding choice and the faith-based education policy. I thought he chose the right riding and was disappointed that voters never gave him credit for keeping his promise — this despite the electorate's oft-expressed complaint about politicians who say one thing and do another.

Now back to the faith-based school funding issue.

One option available to us was simply to reintroduce a flat-dollar tax credit for all parents who sent their children to religious schools. Instead, we decided to explore other options that would provide the fairness we wanted. We asked Alastair Campbell, a very smart policy adviser to former premier Mike Harris, to come up with some options for Tory to consider. Alister did his part, and we then used focus groups to help evaluate the choices.

The choice that resonated best with voters and campaign personnel was to provide funding for faith-based institutions provided they met two key conditions: their curriculum had to be approved by the province;

and they had to be part of the provincial school system and be associated with a public or separate school board

We created the platform document and presented it to a full caucus meeting along with all of the other campaign policies. Overall, the reaction was positive. We prepared for the campaign launch.

However, a comment from an older man in a focus group held in Peterborough stuck in my mind as we organized our campaign. After listening to a description of our faith-based policy, he said, "Let me get this straight, what they are proposing is to pay Muslim kids to make bombs in the basement of the schools. Is that correct?" As the moderator of focus groups, my role is not to answer questions, only to ask questions. I said nothing, but I recall my stomach turning at the comment.

During the summer months leading up to the anticipated October election, our candidates started to report negative reactions they were receiving to our policy. Published polls during that period showed the electorate was divided. The results seemed to vary widely from one polling firm to the next. Some polls showed opposition to the policy as high as 65 percent and support at 32 percent, while other polls showed support at 48 percent and opposition at 44 percent. Our internal polling showed 55 percent opposition and 45 percent support. At the same time, both public polls and our internal polls showed a statistical tie in voter intentions between ourselves and the Liberals, at 38 percent each.

We decided in late July that we needed to release further details about the faith-based school funding policy to address the concerns of some of our candidates.

On July 23, Tory and Frank Klees, our opposition education critic, announced that if we were elected former premier Bill Davis would lead a commission to research and provide recommendations for the inclusion of faith-based schools in Ontario's public school system. This would include identifying best practices in other provinces. The announcement, however, did little to reduce the angst of our candidates.

The campaign officially started on September 10, and our school funding proposal instantly became the number one issue. McGuinty and the Liberals seized advantage of the situation. Each day for most of the first two weeks, McGuinty visited a public school to extol the virtues

I thought the numbers might look larger with glasses. Reviewing the research results with John Tory on election night, 2007.

of the public system and to draw (negative) attention to our policy. He understood the racist undertones behind the opposition of many of those opposed to faith-based school funding, the kind of feelings that had been expressed openly by the man from the Peterborough focus group, and he aggressively drove that point home every day.

We held weekly teleconferences with all of our candidates during the campaign to share information, including research findings. Faith-based funding occupied much of the conversation. Handholding follow-up calls occurred each week.

Despite the fuss, our province-wide voter support held up. On September 13, Ipsos Reid reported the horse race as Liberals 39 percent and PCs 37 percent — a statistical tie. Our own internal polling on September 18–19 found the same thing: a statistical tie with Liberals at 37 percent and PCs at 35 percent.

On September 20, the first and only televised TV debate was held, and Tory acquitted himself very well. Most independent observers thought he won the debate.

The province-wide polling results on September 22–23 again showed no change in voter support — Liberals 37 percent, PCs 35 percent. And our own polling results on September 24, four days after the debate, showed that at 31 percent we were statistically tied with the Liberals (who stood at 32 percent) as being the party with the most momentum in the campaign.

But trouble was brewing within our own ranks.

The week before, our candidate in Bruce-Grey-Owen Sound, MPP Bill Murdoch, had contacted us and said he was going to publicly abandon the faith-based policy. He said he was going to lose his seat over it. I sent Paul Rhodes, our war room chief and a person relatively close to Murdoch, up to his riding to talk to him. Rhodes returned and reported little progress.

I commissioned a poll in Murdoch's riding that week. It showed that Murdoch would win his riding by more than 20 percent. Rhodes provided Murdoch with the poll results. He was not swayed.

"Thanks, Bill Murdoch and Garfield Dunlop." Cartoon showing Ontario PC Party leader John Tory trying to salvage his 2007 Ontario provincial election campaign.

On Monday morning, September 24, Bill Murdoch announced in a media session that he was not supportive of the policy. Like a lemming, MPP Garfield Dunlop from Simcoe North followed suit three hours later.

The voter intention numbers did not change that evening. Neither did the party with the most-momentum numbers. The next day, on September 25, our polling again showed no change in voter intentions, but we started to slide in the standings of the party with the most momentum. Over the next five nights, we went from being tied with the Liberals in momentum to seeing the Liberals take a 10 percent lead — 35 to 25 percent.

My experience with political polling has demonstrated that when the momentum numbers drop for a party, the voter intention numbers will soon follow suit. That is exactly what happened to us. By October 1 our voter intention numbers had dropped significantly: the Liberals now stood at 37 percent and the PCs at 31 percent.

On October 1, we made the decision to announce that, if elected, we would put the policy on faith-based funding to a free vote in the legislature. We knew that this would be perceived as weak leadership, and indeed Tory's personal favourability numbers sagged over the next nine days. But making this announcement was the lesser of two evils. The Murdoch/Dunlop disease was threatening to spread to other candidates.

By the end of that week we were 10 percent down, with the Liberals at 40 percent and the PCs at 30. On election night, October 10, the Liberals won a majority government with 42 percent of the vote; we ended up with 32 percent.

Despite insisting that their seats were at risk, Bill Murdoch was elected in Bruce-Grey-Owen Sound with a plurality of 14 percent, and Garfield Dunlop's advantage was 19 percent. John Tory lost Don Valley West to Kathleen Wynne. Dalton McGuinty was returned to Queen's Park with a majority government thanks mainly to two MPPs who had never heard, did not believe, or could not understand Ronald Reagan's dictum.

* * *

Of course not all elections hinge on large-scale policy issues. Many are won and lost on more local matters. As I mentioned earlier in this book, U.S. Congressman Tip O'Neill famously said that all politics is local. But the strategies that win campaigns are not! In 1995 I found myself in Kyrgyzstan, one of the former Soviet republics, working for an improbable, far-away international client who wanted the backroom political expertise I had accumulated in Canadian campaigns. I discovered that, indeed, good political strategies are not local; they can be applied anywhere. In the next chapter I will describe my experiences over ten years in that new democracy.

Chapter 13

Kyrgyzstan:
A Western Campaign in a New Democracy

This gun's for hire.
— BRUCE SPRINGSTEEN,
"Dancing in the Dark"

I confess I had never heard of Kyrgyzstan before I went there in 1995 to help Askar Akayev fight a presidential election. It is one of the so-called "stans" — rural, impoverished republics in Central Asia that were once part of the Soviet Union. Landlocked Kyrgyzstan is bordered by China to the east, Kazakhstan to the north, Uzbekistan to the west, and Tajikistan to the southwest.

Kyrgyzstan has historically been at the crossroads of several great civilizations, and at one point in its history was part of the Great Silk Road connecting China and Europe. Kyrgyzstan has a population of a little over five million, two-thirds of them being ethnic Kyrgyz, with two significant minorities consisting of Uzbeks and Russians.

From 1936 Kyrgyzstan was a full republic member of the Soviet Union. When the Soviet Union broke up in 1991, Kyrgyzstan became an independent country.

Before I start to recount my political experiences in this developing country, I should introduce the political figures who were important at that time and whose paths I crossed.

Askar Akayev

Prior to becoming president of Kyrgyzstan, Akayev was an academic. This soft-spoken physicist had been the president of the Kyrgyzstan Academy of Sciences and a member of the Parliament of the USSR. He was close to a small group of well-known Russian democrats, including professor Andrei Sakharov, a nuclear physicist (known as the father of the Soviet hydrogen bomb) and later a human rights activist (and winner of the 1975 Nobel Peace Prize), and Anatoly Sobchak, who became the first democratically elected mayor of St. Petersburg and later was a mentor to both Vladimir Putin and Dmitry Medvedev.

After the breakup of the Soviet Union in 1991, two other politicians had contested the presidency of Kyrgyzstan but each had failed to obtain a majority in the first round of voting. According to the rules in place at the time, neither was permitted to leave his name on the ballot for a second round. Akayev put his name forward and was unopposed. He was something of a liberal at heart, and once in office he actively promoted privatization of land and other assets. His administration championed a free press and freedom of speech. By 1995, Western observers saw him as a bright hope for democracy in Central Asia. He cultivated good relations with both the United States and Russia.

Felix Kulov

A Russian-speaking Kyrgyz, he initially trained as a police officer and later held various posts in the national government, including positions of vice-president and prime minister. Kulov was the popular mayor of Bishkek, the capital of Kyrgyzstan, between 1998 and 1999.

Kurmanbek Bakiyev

An ethnic Kypchak (a tribe from Fergana Valley in the south of Kyrgyzstan), Bakiyev was the leader of the Ak Jol opposition party in 2005.

Kamil Baialinov

The press secretary to President Akayev when I first met him, Kamil went on to become Kyrgyzstan's ambassador to Austria and several other countries, and later to the United Nations. He eventually emigrated to Canada.

I would come into contact with each of these political actors between 1995 and 2005.

In November 1995 I found myself in Bishkek, the capital of Kyrgyzstan, presenting the results of recently conducted focus groups to the press secretary and the chief of staff of the president of Kyrgyzstan, Askar Akayev.

Travelling to Kyrgyzstan from Canada in 1995 involved an overnight flight to London's Heathrow Airport, a six-hour layover there, a ten-hour flight to Almaty, the capital of neighbouring Kazakhstan, and from there a four-hour drive by automobile through the Tian Shan mountain range to Bishkek. Total elapsed time: twenty-seven hours.

The format of the meeting was pretty standard. I presented an overview of my findings, covering the mood of the electorate, their hopes, dreams, and fears, and their impressions of their political leaders. I concluded with some recommendations for President Akayev's upcoming campaign for re-election. (The election was scheduled for Christmas Eve, 1995. The timing would be unusual in Western Christian countries, but two-thirds of the citizens of Kyrgyzstan are Muslim and do not observe Christmas, and many others are Orthodox Christians who use the Julian calendar.)

While the format was standard, the setting of the meeting was anything but. I was sitting naked in a sauna eating grilled chicken and drinking Miller Beer while presenting my findings from the focus groups. The sauna was located in the officers' barracks of a military camp. In the background I could hear cadets singing martial songs as they prepared to call it a day.

I recall thinking how surreal this picture was and asking myself, "What am I doing here?" This was to be the first of a number of surreal moments for me in this country.

A little background on how I came to be there.

Charles McMillan, a policy adviser to former prime minister Brian Mulroney, was a professor at York University in Toronto, and over the previous year he had opened up a business school in Bishkek in co-operation with the Kyrgyz government.

Charles had happened to meet Kamil Baialinov and Miriam Akayeva, wife of President Akayev, on a flight out of Washington, D.C. They told him of Miriam's meeting with First Lady Hillary Clinton and mentioned that Miriam had asked if Hillary could suggest a good Western campaign manager who could help her husband in his upcoming presidential run. Charles told them that he had someone to suggest from Canada. Someone who could help them provide an open and honest democratic election — with pollsters, political ads, buttons, and all the other bells and whistles that Western voters are familiar with.

I received a telephone call from Charles shortly thereafter. Would I be interested in helping Askar Akayev get re-elected in December, McMillan asked? If so, he wanted me to meet Kamil Baialinov, the president's press secretary, who was going to be in Toronto for a couple of days. I was intrigued, but I had already made plans to be at our family cottage in Ontario's Kawartha Lakes district that weekend.

Two days later, though, I was looking over the back of our in-board motorboat to see how Kamil was doing on water skis on Jack Lake. Our guest had gotten up on his second try and was hanging on for dear life. He had snow skied before, but this was a very new experience for him. As I watched him struggling to stay up, refusing to fall, I decided this was one tough and determined individual. Later, Charlie, Kamil, and I discussed how I might be able to assist in the re-election campaign. Plans were made for my visit to Bishkek in November.

I obviously did not speak either Kyrgyz or Russian (the working language in Kyrgyzstan), but a colleague of mine at Goldfarb Consultants, Vladimir Levkov, a computer data specialist, was a Russian-speaking Latvian. He agreed to help translate our discussions. Vladimir assisted me in each of the campaigns I helped with over the next ten years. He and I enjoyed our visits, and despite the volatility of the political situation in the country we generally felt safe there — for the presidential election in 2000, a referendum in 2003, and a parliamentary election in

2005. Regardless, we were assigned an armed bodyguard for the duration of our 2003 referendum.

On our first visit, I attended a set of focus groups in Bishkek for which I had trained a moderator to lead the discussion. The meetings were held in an unheated government building. Huddled over a heater in an adjoining room, I watched the video of the session being conducted by the moderator. Seated beside me was an interpreter who provided simultaneous translation of the proceedings. At times I felt that the sound of my knees knocking together from the cold would drown out the voice of the interpreter.

On the same trip Vladimir and I trained a large number of students to conduct interviews for a quantitative poll to complement and verify the findings of the focus groups.

Kamil had organized the recruitment of these students. They were eager to be part of a group helping the president and were anxious for the money they would be paid. Each of the interviewers was paid five dollars per shift. (Kamil assured me that this made great economic sense for the students, as they only received eight dollars per month as their living allowance; Kyrgyz physicians at the time were paid on average thirty dollars per month.)

One of the initial challenges in conducting a telephone poll in Kyrgyzstan was to determine whether the results were accurate. In North America, where nearly 95 percent of people have telephones, pollsters can be reasonably assured that if the sample is drawn properly (that is, randomly), the results will fall within the margin of error determined by the size of the sample. At that time in Kyrgyzstan only 15 percent of the population had telephones. I assumed that these individuals would be opinion leaders and might reflect the views of the masses. But I needed to verify that assumption.

While the students were conducting interviews by phone both in Bishkek and across the rest of Kyrgyzstan, Vladimir and I trained a squad of students to conduct interviews on the streets of the capital using a paper questionnaire and a clipboard.

Three days later my assumption was verified. The vote results of the phoning and the on-street interviews in Bishkek were within the margin of error.

There were other challenges in conducting research in Kyrgyzstan. Obtaining phone lists from which to draw a sample required the resources of the president's office, and Kamil and his band of helpers arranged to have thirty-five telephones installed in a large boardroom at the university from which we had recruited the students.

Vladimir trained a data entry person to input the poll results into the data files and produced the statistical tables I needed to prepare the report for the president. Kamil arranged for our PowerPoint presentation to be translated into Russian.

Vladimir, Kamil, and I presented the results to the president in his office in the White House, the seat of government in Kyrgyzstan. The polling indicated that the president would win in a landslide. His opponents were not well thought of, and he had a favourable approval rating.

A media campaign was still needed, however, so the insights from both the polling and the focus groups were put to use in creating ads that Kamil produced, as well as other communications materials. One of the major buys of such materials was plastic shopping bags.

At the time the country had very little infrastructure to support the retail industry. Particularly noticeable was the lack of any packaging or plastic bags for shoppers, most of whom took their purchases home wrapped in newspapers. Kamil and his campaign team saw an opportunity. Süleyman Demirel, the president of Turkey, had indicated a willingness to help Akayev win re-election and, as the campaign started, half a million plastic bags adorned with Akayev's face, his name, and the campaign slogan were delivered from Istanbul.

As Kamil recalled later, the first distribution of those bags was done by thieves from the airport who pilfered thousands of them from the cargo plane, thinking that they were valuable goods. I would see those very simple bags being carried on the street many times over the next few years.

I returned to Toronto in early December and watched the results with some satisfaction on Christmas Eve 1995. Akayev received 74 percent of the vote, reasonably close to the 81 percent predicted in the final survey we had completed on December 22. This satisfaction was somewhat diminished a few years later, however, when Kamil confided that the Akayev campaign had made sure that the votes in the ballot boxes were counted to more or less coincide with my vote projections.

2000 PRESIDENTIAL ELECTION

The March 2000 email from Kamil in Vienna was cryptic: "The situation is not so simple as it was in 1995."

Following the 1995 election, President Akayev had appointed Kamil as Kyrgyzstan's ambassador to Austria, the Czech Republic, Hungary, Slovakia, and Israel. Now he was bringing him back from Vienna to Bishkek to help position himself for the 2000 election. And he asked for me to be involved again. Kamil wrote, "We are in need of your head, your knowledge and reliance of a victory. The manager of the campaign shall be I. The head will be you."

The first poll, taken in April 2000, and a set of focus groups that were conducted shortly afterward confirmed Kamil's prediction of a tough election campaign. Akayev's voter support was in the mid-30 percent range. He was statistically tied with Felix Kulov, a popular former mayor of Bishkek. There was a huge appetite for change in the country.

Toasting the numbers on the Great Silk Road. I met with Kamil Baialinov and Vladimir Levkov to brief President Akayev (to my left) on my research results in Bishkek, Kyrgyzstan, in 2000.

I tested some actions that Akayev might take to improve his standing in the polls. In my presentation to the president before I left Bishkek on this first visit, I suggested a plan designed to allow him to "own" change before the election scheduled for October that year. The main changes I suggested were to:

- Make Russian the second official language of the country
- Introduce tax changes benefiting small businesses to create more jobs
- Make changes to his team ahead of the election campaign
- Increase the support for pensioners
- Make a number of democratic changes, including direct elections for mayor of Bishkek and the heads of the oblasts (provinces)

Akayev then introduced the first two changes on the above list. We conducted polls in May, July, and August of that year. Each of these polls showed an improvement in Akayev's voter support. By August his support was at 66 percent of the decided voters.

While my plan may have helped, two other events definitely improved the president's chances.

First, his main opponent, Felix Kulov, a Russian-speaking Kyrgyz, failed the Kyrgyzstan language test required for all presidential candidates. He was not allowed to register as a candidate.

Second, Kulov was arraigned on corruption charges. These charges were laid by the Kyrgyz KGB; while many politicians may have had suspicions about their origin, there was never any proof that the president was involved in the decision.

On October 29, 2000, Akayev won re-election handily over five other candidates, with over 76 percent of the vote. International election monitors described the process as failing to meet international standards. This was no great surprise to me, as my August polling had found that only 28 percent of the people believed the election would be conducted in an honest and open fashion. The seeds of discontent with the political process would eventually come back to haunt Akayev and his family in 2005.

Kamil told me that he was present when the chief of staff opened the safe in the president's office and withdrew the U.S. cash to cover my consulting fee. He counted it out in front of Kamil, who recalls stopping the counting when he noticed a few $100 bills had what appeared to be blood stains on them. He suggested it would not be appropriate for me to be given that "bloody money" to carry back to Canada. Kamil told me that in 2000 the president had lost many of his rich supporters and that this money had been collected from a number of sources, including revenue officers and criminals.

In January 2001, following the election, Kulov was found guilty of corruption and sentenced to seven years in prison by a military court. He spent four years in jail and was released by the people following the First Kyrgyz Revolution in 2005. Ironically, before the revolution broke out President Akayev had wanted to release Kulov and appoint him acting prime minister — but events overtook the president and the country.

Kamil and I would cross paths with Kulov one more time.

2003 REFERENDUM

President Akayev decided to call a referendum to obtain approval for a number of changes to the country's constitution. He embarked on two parallel tracks. One was public; the other was private.

On the public track Akayev convened a series of meetings of a forty-member Constitutional Council in August and September of 2002. The formation of this group was widely seen as a positive step forward for the country, as it included both pro-government and opposition political figures. On October 2 a final report was published on the council's draft amendments to the constitution.

On October 17, the president issued a decree that the draft amendments should be published in all newspapers and public meetings held to explain the proposals. The public would be encouraged to submit their ideas for changes.

On January 2, 2003, the president issued a further decree: since many of the public suggestions had differed from the Constitutional Council's proposals, he would create an "experts' group." On January 13 the experts' group reported with a final set of constitutional amendments (with a number of new amendments), and the president issued a further decree that a referendum would be held on February 2, 2003.

Meanwhile, as all of this was happening in the public arena, President Akayev had his own "experts' panel" working on a second, private track. He had become a strong believer in public opinion research, and he wanted his own information from the public through the use of qualitative and quantitative research.

In August 2002 President Akayev put out a call for me once again.

Air travel from Toronto to Bishkek had improved greatly since my first visit in 1995. Manas Airport in Bishkek was now an international airport and received flights regularly from Asia and Europe. Another significant change had occurred in the aftermath of the terrorists' destruction of the World Trade Center in New York on September 11, 2001. Manas Airport was now being used by the Americans and its allies for military operations and strikes in Afghanistan. Our arrival at the airport in the early hours of the morning coincided with the roar of French Mirage jets flying out on patrol.

I met with the president, and he described his plans for revising the constitution. He emphasized to me that he was mainly interested in making positive changes and not in changing the constitution for his own purposes, such as allowing himself to run for a third five-year term in 2005.

I conducted a small number of focus groups in mid- September. With Vladimir's assistance I conducted the first of a series of large quantitative polls designed primarily to test the reaction to the referendum and to the changes that the president was contemplating. I reported to Akayev that the voters had a very positive view of the use of a referendum and many of the proposed changes. There was also strong support for him to stay in office until 2005 and serve out his term as president.

I also found that the people generally wanted the president rather than the parliament (known as the Jogorku Kenesh) to have more powers.

Two further waves of research and a final set of focus groups were conducted in October and November. I reported that there had been a continued improvement in the president's approval rating over the previous three months. Conversely, there had been a steady decrease in the overall impression of the MPs during that same time.

I reported that reducing the number of MPs, moving to a one-tier parliament from Kyrgyzstan's bicameral system, and giving some additional powers to the president were among the most positive changes that he could make to the constitution. The people also said they wanted a simple referendum vote: "one question, one answer."

During the final four weeks, Akayev made a number of unilateral modifications to his proposed package of changes on the basis of our research findings. Rather than one question, Akayev decided to have two simple questions.

Our numbers suggested strong 90 percent–plus approval for the two questions: the first on the package of changes to the constitution, and the second on support for Akayev to stay in office until 2005. (Akayev also included in this latter question a provision for absolute and permanent immunity for himself and his family when his term ended.)

On February 2, 2003, voters turned out to overwhelmingly endorse the constitutional amendments, with 89 percent in favour, and support President Akayev's intention to carry on until 2005.

By this time members of Akayev's family had taken over many of the country's more profitable businesses and were thinking about ruling the country on their own terms. It would be the beginning of the end of Akayev's political career.

2005 PARLIAMENTARY ELECTIONS

In the fall of 2004 the president's two adult children contacted me. His daughter Bermet Akayeva and his son Aidar Akayev had spent the previous year organizing a new political party named Alga Kyrgyzstan ("Forward Kyrgyzstan") with the intent of fielding a large number of candidates in the anticipated 2005 parliamentary elections. They had invested substantially in this effort, spending money in numerous communities to build playgrounds, community centres, and other infrastructure. They wanted me to assist them by organizing research to support their election efforts.

Vladimir and I returned to Bishkek.

We conducted a number of studies that indicated the new party would likely elect the largest number of members in the new parliament. I recall that during our initial meeting discussing the plans with the president, I expressed my concern about the perception of having too much power in the hands of the one family. I also recall that I did not pursue the topic any further after that initial meeting.

The electoral district studies showed that Alga Kyrgyzstan would indeed do very well in the March elections, perhaps too well. Under the election rules, a second round of voting was held in each of the districts where the leading candidate did not achieve a majority of the votes cast in the first round. While there were no official results of the balloting — the final results of this election were overwhelmed by subsequent events known as the "Tulip Revolution," media reports suggest that the opposition won just six seats out of seventy-five. International observers and media were very critical of the conduct of both rounds of balloting, describing them as falling well short of international standards.

In the months before the election, the opposition had decided that Akayev's next move would be to want to become president for life with the support of the parliament that would now be controlled by his children. This controversial election was about to blow the country apart. On the basis of my research findings I told Akayev that a significant number of citizens claimed they would participate in a protest, and that he should be concerned.

I had left Kyrgyzstan some two weeks in advance of round one of the election. I faced a rather pleasant dilemma, though. We had conducted such a large number of electoral district studies that at the conclusion of the project I was faced with a dilemma: how to get $150,000 in U.S. one hundred-dollar Ben Franklin bills back home to Canada. Rather than trust the banking system, I decided to put the money in my briefcase and fly home with the cash.

Only when the airline attendant passed out the Canadian landing card did I see a new requirement to declare cash amounts of $10,000 or more. I completed the declaration and was diverted to the customs screening area at Toronto's Pearson International Airport. I remember the amazed look on the customs officer's face as I told him of the sum of money in the briefcase. "You are a big man," he told me, shaking his head. I managed to persuade the customs officer that all was legit. And so I was able to bring the money home.

Soon after, I was vacationing in Guatemala with my wife. On Easter weekend I turned on CNN and watched as the Tulip Revolution unfolded in Bishkek and as my client, President Akayev, abandoned the White House just as it was being stormed by a mob of protesters. He fled the country. To this day, Akayev is living in Moscow under Vladimir Putin's supervision.

The political system in Kyrgyzstan was very different from those of other democratic societies. I recall the words of an elderly Kyrgyz man during a focus group I conducted in 2000. He said that he was going to vote for Akayev because "he has already stolen enough and Akayev (unlike a new president) will not have to steal any more."

There were rumours in Bishkek in 2005 that the United States government had provided the main opposition leader, Kurmanbek Bakiyev, together with Roza Otunbayeva, a former minister of Foreign Affairs who would later be acting president, with a large sum of money that was spent on recruiting and liquoring-up a crowd prior to the storming of the White House. The Americans had become upset with Akayev, who they felt was too pro-Russian. This was despite the fact that Akayev was allowing the United States the use of Manas Airport (albeit at a steep rent) from which to patrol the skies over Afghanistan post 9/11.

After the Tulip Revolution, Bakiyev was quickly appointed acting president and prime minister by the Supreme Council of Kyrgyzstan.

KYRGYZSTAN 2005, POST-REVOLUTION

In April 2005, one month after the Tulip Revolution, we were once again recruited to do research in Kyrgyzstan. This time it was in support of

Felix Kulov, who had been released from prison during the revolution by the crowd of protestors. Kamil Baialinov had maintained good relations with Kulov and believed that he, not Bakiyev, would make the best president. Upon his release Kulov had been appointed coordinator of law enforcement and security services by Bakiyev. Kulov then announced his intention to stand as a candidate for president in the elections scheduled for July 10.

We conducted a large quantitative poll for Kulov. The results showed deep divisions in the country. Kulov and Bakiyev each would receive 50 percent of the vote in a presidential election, with Kulov winning the north of the country and Bakiyev the south. In mid-May we presented the results to Kulov, who arrived at the meeting with two political scientists from Moscow. He listened with interest but was noncommittal in his reaction to the findings.

Three hours after he left the meeting, he announced publicly that he would not be a candidate for president. He further announced that he would be supporting Bakiyev, who later won the election easily.

Kamil told me that he had learned later that the two purported political scientists from Moscow in fact were spies, and they had been trying to convince Kulov that he had no chance to win the presidency. Putin had already decided that Bakiyev was his choice. Kulov was informed that his continued candidacy would not end well for him and his supporters.

Bakiyev then named Kulov as his prime minister, an appointment that was confirmed by the Jogorku Kenesh in September. I left Kyrgyzstan the day after our meeting with Kulov, and the two spies have not returned since.

Bakiyev turned out to be a poor investment for the United States, as a few years later he asked the Americans to leave Manas Airport. Bakiyev was later forced from office by a second revolution, in which a large number of protesters were killed after he allegedly issued orders for government troops to use force against the demonstrators.

Today Kurmanbek Bakiyev lives in exile in Belarus. In 2013 a Kyrgyz court sentenced him in absentia to twenty-four years in jail for abuse of power. His brother Zhanysh, who led the country's security services, was given a life term for crimes including the murder of a close friend of Kamil's. That was Medet Sadyrkulov, a one-time chief of staff for Bakiyev, who had fallen out with the ruthless brothers.

Despite the deficiencies in democracy during the Akayev era in Kyrgyzstan, I have generally positive impressions of Akayev himself. He made many efforts to transform the country from a Soviet communist state to a democracy. Respondents at focus groups would praise the fact that they had freedom of speech (as evidenced by their attendance at these focus groups and their ability to speak freely) and a free press. He was also largely able to control the ethnic tensions in the country between the north and the south, where a significant minority of Uzbeks lived. And his final act as he fled the White House was to order that no weapons be used against his people.

Today, Kamil sees Akayev as a decent man who found himself in the wrong place at the wrong time:

> Akayev's story is the tragic story of a very good man who accidentally got big power. He sincerely wanted to build an open and democratic country.
>
> In Gorbachev and Yeltsin's period Russia had started to open its doors to the world. Many experts thought that with one more step Russia would become a normal developed democratic European country.
>
> Akayev and I mistakenly believed in Russia and its democratic future. When other Asian leaders were building their autocracies, we tried to integrate with Russia — from politics, economy and ending with cultural ties. We even made Russian the second official language. I can see now that it was our greatest mistake. Kyrgyzstan became the Russian satellite it is today because of us. Akayev strongly believed that Russia would be our only locomotive that would take our small and modest car into the future — into Europe.

While we were in our illusions, the neighbors built their successful Asian dictatorships. We became the only democratic island in an ocean of Asian tyranny.

When Putin took over in Russia, Akayev lost his last hope to build a better future for Kyrgyzstan. He lowered his hands and lost interest in ruling the state. He was replaced from his duties by his family and other sorts of charlatans.

I had very interesting conversations with Akayev at that time. I told him, that after the election I was going to leave Kyrgyzstan, because after Putin's leadership we had no future at all.

(We both knew very well who Putin was and what role he played in Saint Petersburg and later in Moscow.) Anatoly Sobchak was the mayor of Saint Petersburg and a close friend of Akayev's and was also a mentor to Putin. We met Putin at drinking meetings with Sobchak many times. We had no doubt who we were dealing with.

Akayev asked me "What about me?" I told him that he had to find an elegant way to finish his presidency in a couple of years (before the 2005 election). Only this would save him from a revolution and shame. If he left with dignity, he would have entered history as a reformer.

When the revolution occurred, Akayev was unable to use force and weapons. He was a good man, not a murderer or tyrant. Such people can't rule in Asia. They are too decent for that.

In the end Akayev was forced to leave the country. Putin provided a prop aircraft and security. Putin had found common cause with Bakiyev and, as Kamil so aptly describes it, "Bakiyev then turned his ass to America and his front to Russia."

I still regard my experience in Kyrgyzstan politics with Askar Akeyev as a positive, despite the fact that in the end, and despite his efforts, the country mainly turned away from the democracy that he intended it to be. He was and is a decent man.

I learned that research can be used in the Third World as well as in established democracies. If the questions and the methodology are correct, then people everywhere enjoy being asked for their opinions, even in a new democracy on the Great Silk Road — a land route for traders and travellers from the Far East to Europe and a new market for Canadian campaign techniques, including market research.

Chapter 14

Observations and Reflections

This is my truth. Tell me yours.
— ANEURIN BEVAN,
Welsh politician (1897–1960)

This rollicking ride through politics is almost finished. I hope you have enjoyed the journey through Canada and beyond, to the United Kingdom and Kyrgyzstan, and the lessons and stories, many of which have never before been told in public.

As I come to the end of this book, I have some observations and reflections to make on my journey.

The first should come as no surprise. It is that most candidates win or lose campaigns on their own merits. The tools in the campaign manager's tool kit are important, but they are there to support the campaign and to enhance the candidate's chances, little more.

It was Brian Mulroney in 1988 whom Canadians trusted most on free trade.

It was Rob Ford in 2010 who Torontonians felt understood their values and their anger at the city hall establishment.

It was Joe Clark in 2000 who made the pivotal decision to run as a candidate in Calgary Centre, a gutsy move that helped to keep his struggling Progressive Conservative Party alive.

It was Justin Trudeau in 2012 who gambled that, if he stepped into a boxing ring in a charity match against the heavily favoured Senator Patrick Brazeau, he could demonstrate that he was more than just the son of a famous politician.

It was David Miller, a Toronto city councillor in 2001, who established his name when he braved death threats against his family by opposing a night club project on behalf of his constituents, and who led the charge at city hall to uncover a computer leasing scandal.

It was John Crosbie in 1983 who campaigned in support of free trade while most of his party opposed it.

Their names were on the ballot, not those of their campaign managers.

My second observation is that while politics is the easiest business for a candidate to get into, it can be the toughest to exit from. During the last forty-plus years I have watched only a handful of politicians exit politics well. These include Bill Davis, Joe Clark, Brian Mulroney, Peter Lougheed, David Miller, John Crosbie, Mike Harris, Peter MacKay, and Brian Peckford.

Most others did not do it well. Some stayed too long, perhaps because they could not find the right time to leave.

I had a glimpse into the thinking of Stephen Harper in May 2015 when he spoke in Nova Scotia after Peter MacKay announced that he was quitting active politics. I had a sense that Harper wanted to leave, too, but there were unseen forces at play. "No matter how much you enjoy being part of this great ride we are on, the time comes when you want to get off," he said. "Even though this ride never actually stops, getting off is never easy."

Harper was prophetic. It was not easy for him. He did not exit well.

My third observation is that there has been a substantial decrease in the amount of civility in politics since I first became involved in the 1970s. Much has been written about this trend in both the United States and Canada.

Wall Street Journal columnist Peggy Noonan wrote a story about Ronald Reagan entitled *When Character Was King*. In describing the fortieth president of the United States, Noonan wrote: "The secret of his success was no secret at all. It was his character — his courage, his kindness, his persistence, his honesty … that was the most important element of his success." Looking at the political sewer that is Washington, D.C., today, one cannot help but be struck by the lack of character, courage, kindness, and honesty among some elected representatives. Their lack of maturity and sophistication is galling.

Peter's MacKay's part in uniting the right was a rare example of political courage. Author with Peter MacKay as he settles into the private sector.

In early 2015 Laurie Hawn, the Conservative MP from Edmonton Centre, a sixty-six-year-old former lieutenant-colonel in the Royal Canadian Air Force, commented on his decision not to seek re-election. His military background meant that he had been involved in some of the most heated debates on matters such as the torture of Afghan detainees, the treatment of veterans, and the purchase of new fighter jets. "It's not a secret that Parliament has been combative and it should be that way. But it should be measured, it should be respectful, it should be rational. I think we've gotten away from that to a greater extent than I would like."

Hawn continued: "I've always said, the opposition members are not stupid people, we're all here for the same reason, we all came to Ottawa to make a positive difference and we all want to get essentially to the same destination. We argue about the road we're on to get there."

Other MPs and leaders, from one-time Reform Party leader Preston Manning to NDP leader Jack Layton, have made similar observations over the years.

Perhaps I am wrong, but I do not think it was always thus. Let me offer just two small personal examples.

I was meeting with John Crosbie just prior to Christmas 1985 in his House of Commons office. Crosbie was at the time the federal minister of justice. In the middle of our conversation John's secretary interrupted to say that former prime minister Pierre Trudeau was returning his call. John explained to me that he had put in a call to Trudeau that morning to give him a heads-up that the Mulroney government was going to publicly release some of Trudeau's Cabinet documents in the week between Christmas and New Year's. John said he needed to take the call. He picked up the phone. His opening comments to Trudeau in French were simply, "Bonjour. Comment ça va?" I could hear Trudeau's gales of laughter at the sound of Crosbie's unanticipated Newfoundland French echoing off the high ceiling in the office. The two men bantered back and forth. Trudeau asked Crosbie how the opposition was treating him; Crosbie replied that they were being as obstreperous as all other previous opposition parties. There was more laughter on the other end of the line. During those few minutes I had a very real insight into the relationship between two men who seemed to respect each other despite being on opposite sides of many political issues.

A few years before, in early 1978, I had experienced another example of civility from the late Liberal Senator Keith Davey. On the morning that it was announced to the public that I would be ending my five-year stint as national director of the PC Party of Canada, I received a call from Keith. He wanted to congratulate me and thank me for my efforts in the political process. He enquired what I was planning to do next and arranged for me to meet with three companies in Toronto where he felt there could be some job opportunities I should consider.

These two examples of across-the-aisle civility do not appear to be the norm in today's politics, where personal attacks and extreme partisanship so often dominate. I believe this is part of the reason why more and more voters are becoming disengaged from the political system.

* * *

As I wrote this book I had time to reflect on what I have accomplished over the last four decades and what differences I have made as a result of leaving IBM in 1973 to involve myself in politics full-time.

If I had stayed at IBM my legacy would have been measured by the number of computers I sold.

What can I look back on today as my accomplishments in politics?

First, there are the changes that I contributed to inside the profession of politics.

I have already described my start in politics as part of the Dirty Dozen — the first group of advance men in Canada to plan political leaders' travel in a professional manner. We used a book called *The Advance Man,* published in 1971 by Jerry Bruno, as our bible. Bruno's book is based on his work for many Democratic candidates, including President John F. Kennedy. Bruno advanced Kennedy's final trip to Dallas in 1963, planning the president's movements in precise detail. A week later, on the day when Kennedy was in Dallas, Bruno was preparing the following week's trip to another city. The plan that Bruno had laid for Dallas called for the use of an automobile with a covered top — a plans that was changed at the last minute. The president was travelling in an open convertible when he was assassinated. We took Jerry's lessons to heart, realizing how crucial each and every detail can be in preparing a day on the tour.

As national director of the Progressive Conservative Party in 1974, and with Hugh Segal's assistance, I talked the PC Canada Fund directors into putting up $50,000 to start a direct-mail campaign to take advantage of the generous tax credits in the new Election Expenses Act. Ours was the first party to do so, and the success of that program gave successive Conservative leaders the financial wherewithal to compete successfully for many elections. Other parties have since followed our example. The only downside for me personally has been the number of Canadians who curse the person who started direct-mail and telephone fundraising solicitations for political parties, calls that seem inevitably to come at dinner time.

In 1976 I introduced telephone canvassing on a large scale to identify voter intentions during the Ottawa-Carleton by-election that had been called to replace Liberal Cabinet minister John Turner. I had met Mary Ellen Miller, a U.S. political consultant, who was proposing to do some work for the Ontario PC Party. As a trial run in Canada we agreed to test the system during the federal by-election. We set up a phone bank in the library at party headquarters, staffed it with volunteers, and called every voter in the riding. The results of our calling showed that our candidate, Jean Pigott, would win with approximately 50 percent of the vote. That was exactly what she received on election night.

All was not smooth sailing, though. George Hees, one of our veteran MPs, lived in the riding. George called and asked to see me in my office. He said that he had been receiving a number of complaints about our phone calls and the script that asked people how they were going to vote. He said voting is a personal, private matter. After my probing, George told me he had received just six complaints from his neighbours. I suggested that out of some 25,000 calls we had made this was a pretty minor issue. Then I asked George whether he thought those six voters might be Liberals. George became a big believer in phone banks after Pigott's victory.

Another initiative in which I played a role was the uniting of the two right-of-centre parties the Canadian Alliance and the Progressive Conservatives. Following the 2000 federal election, it became clear that as long as there were two parties on the right it would be difficult, if not impossible, to beat the Liberals.

I had stayed in touch with Joe Clark and his staff after the 2000 election, and in early 2001 Clark invited me to a meeting at a small boutique hotel in Montreal. It was a secret all-day session with four members of the Canadian Alliance. Attending the meeting from their side were Chuck Strahl, Canadian Alliance MP from British Columbia, and Ray Speaker, a former Reform Party MP, and two others. Clark, I, and two others represented the PC Party. Clark knew the members of our party were not yet ready for a merger of equals, but he felt that with the disappointing results for the Canadian Alliance in 2000 there were some interim steps that might be palatable to both sides. He was convinced that he was better positioned than Stockwell Day, the Canadian Alliance leader, to unite the right under his leadership; the Alliance was in disarray, and by June 2001 of that year thirteen MPs had left their caucus. The Montreal meeting was but the first of many informal sessions that took place with a number of different people over the following months.

By July 2001 the defecting Alliance MPs had chosen to sit in the House of Commons as the Democratic Representative Caucus (DRC). A joint meeting of some eighty Canadian Alliance and PC Party members at Mont-Tremblant, Quebec, was decided for August 2001.

I was asked to conduct research regarding co-operation between the two parties and/or the parties' merger. Those findings were presented to the Mont-Tremblant meeting. A number of decisions came out of this meeting. It was agreed to form a parliamentary coalition between the DRC and the PC Party. It was also agreed to set up two working groups — one on democratic reform and one to answer the question "Where do we go from here?"

I conducted additional research on democratic reform, and it was presented to the Progressive Conservatives' national council in September.

The co-operation in Parliament lasted until April 2002. In the meantime Stockwell Day resigned and Stephen Harper became the new leader of the Canadian Alliance. The tensions in the parliamentary coalition between the Tories and the Canadian Alliance never disappeared — each harboured a different vision of the end game for the united right. For example, who would be in control? Co-operation started to unravel over the decision of the combined alliance in Parliament not to oppose the Liberal budget in 2002. Scott Brison, the group's finance critic, would not vote against the Liberal budget in parliament. He felt that any opposition to the budget would result in the voters in Atlantic Canada believing that the PC Party would give away their benefits. The Canadian Alliance members of the coalition took that as a signal that the PCs were not really conservative, and some time later all but one of the DRC MPs returned to the Alliance with its new leader, Harper. The right remained divided. Harper had no interest in forming a new party. He thought that he was in the best position to unite the right under the Canadian Alliance banner because he had the largest number of MPs.

Joe Clark, realizing that the opportunity to consolidate the right under his leadership had passed, stepped down in August 2002, and in May 2003 Peter MacKay was elected leader of the PC Party. Just before that leadership convention a by-election was held in the southern Ontario riding of Perth-Middlesex. I conducted the research for that campaign, and PC candidate Gary Schellenberger won decisively. This was a pivotal moment. The Canadian Alliance's failure to win a by-election in Ontario convinced Stephen Harper that a new combined party was needed.

I managed Peter MacKay's successful campaign for the leadership of the Progressive Conservative Party in May, immediately after the Ontario by-election, a victory achieved with a deal that MacKay made with third-place candidate David Orchard.

Bob Plamondon, in his 2004 book *Full Circle,* describes the events that took place following the release of the results in the first round of balloting in that PC leadership contest. MacKay was first, Jim Prentice was second, and David Orchard was third with roughly 25 percent of the vote. As Bob recounts, the individual who was key to putting MacKay and David Orchard into a hotel room to discuss the future of the party was a senator from New Brunswick, Noël Kinsella. Noël had worked with Orchard previously and had gained his trust.

Earlier in that week our tracking of delegates indicated the Orchard would win 25 percent of the votes, and that while he could not win, he and his supporters would decide the final outcome. I arranged to meet with Grant Orchard, David's brother, in order to open up the lines of communication between the Orchard and MacKay campaigns. I felt that it was a cordial meeting — a good first step.

Kinsella and MacKay met in a hotel room with David and Grant Orchard and reviewed the agreement that Orchard had prepared on a sheet of paper. Part of the agreement was to clean up national head-quarters, replace the national director, have a blue-ribbon commission review the Canada-U.S. and North American free trade agreements, and put environmental protection at the forefront of the party's policy-making process. But the last element of the arrangement — and the one that was most important to Orchard — was that there would be no talks about merger or joint candidates with the Canadian Alliance, and that in the next election the PC Party would run candidates in all 301 ridings.

Peter modified Orchard's piece of paper with respect to the composi-tion of the blue-ribbon commission and left the room to consult with me and Bill Pristanski, who was our campaign chair. We both gave Peter the same advice. I said, "This deal will be trouble for you in the future, but it's the right thing to do. You can't win without it."

Peter went back into the room and signed the deal.

Peter MacKay took a lot of heat and personal attacks for making the deal, and then for breaking it later to unite the right-of-centre parties. In my view he demonstrated courage that is rare in politics today. He gave up his immediate leadership ambitions for the sake of a united right-of-centre party that shortly thereafter became the Conservative government of Canada under Harper.

The rest is history. Serious negotiations between the two parties then took place, and an agreement to form a new party was reached. While my role in this process was minor, I was involved at several points during the long process that led to the Liberals finally being defeated in 2006.

I have also reflected on the three major policy issues that I was involved in during a number of campaigns that helped make real differences — some positive and some negative — in the lives of Canadians.

The first was the Canada-Newfoundland Atlantic Accord that was passed in 1985. A number of Progressive Conservatives deserve the credit for this piece of legislation that has transformed Newfoundland and Labrador into a "have" province. Brian Mulroney, Joe Clark, John Crosbie, and Brian Peckford each played key roles. I was involved with all of them during the period 1979–85, and I take some pride in assisting in their achievement. In 1996, while in Newfoundland helping PC leader Lynn Verge prepare for a provincial election, I found myself in Clarenville, in the eastern part of the island. An off-shore drilling rig for Hibernia was being built there. It was twilight, and I could see the lights on the rig and the lights in the town where five thousand Newfoundlanders were working on the construction of the rig, thanks to the accord. I felt a shiver go up my spine as I observed this scene. It is not often that one sees such tangible, visible results in politics.

The second major policy issue that my candidates campaigned on was the Canada-U.S. Free Trade Agreement. John Crosbie championed the cause, and Brian Mulroney made it come to fruition. I view my role in implementing the Free Trade Agreement with pride, as it demonstrated that Canada was an outward-looking and confident nation. The economic benefits for Canadians to date have been as advertised.

The third major policy issue that I was on the fringes of with two of my campaigns was the Meech Lake Accord. In April 1987 Brian Mulroney met with the ten provincial premiers and agreed upon a package of proposed amendments to the Constitution of Canada, in an attempt to persuade the government of Quebec to recognize the 1982 Constitution that it had refused to sign.

I will not describe all of the events that occurred between 1987 and 1989, but in essence the accord failed because it was not ratified by two of the legislatures — Manitoba and Newfoundland and Labrador. There had been a change in government in each province since Mulroney and the premiers had reached agreement at Meech Lake. I had a role in each of those provinces that indirectly led to the failure of the accord.

In Manitoba in 1986 I had been pressed into duty as Progressive Conservative Gary Filmon's campaign manager at the last minute. Filmon lost that election narrowly to the NDP under Howard Pawley. I kept in touch with Gary after the election and helped him to recruit Greg Lyle, a young Social Credit organizer from British Columbia, to be his chief of staff. In early 1988 the province was thrown into another, unexpected election because of the resignation of a government MLA. Filmon talked to his caucus about bringing me back to run the campaign. He encountered resistance from those who thought that as a Quebecker and former member of Mulroney's campaign team I would be sympathetic to Quebec's point of view during this period when the Meech Lake Accord was such a prominent issue. He called to say that it would not work out to have me run the campaign. Instead, he appointed one of his MLAs as campaign manager.

The PC Party entered the 1988 race with a significant lead. The campaign did not go well, although Filmon was able to scrape through with a minority government. While Filmon personally eventually agreed to support Meech Lake, he was unable to gain the support of his minority legislature and could only watch as Elijah Harper held a feather in his hand in the chamber and refused to allow Meech Lake to come to a vote. I am not suggesting I could have made a difference to the outcome of the election, but I have never encountered an elected politician who could manage a campaign. A politician has a very different skill set from a campaign manager.

The second province to scuttle the Meech Lake Accord was Newfoundland and Labrador. In March 1989 Tom Rideout won the leadership of the Progressive Conservative Party of Newfoundland and Labrador, replacing Brian Peckford. Within a month he called a provincial election. I had managed Tom's leadership bid, and he asked me to run the provincial election. I returned to St. John's. Just as the election started I developed an infection in my liver from some sort of amoeba and had to fly back to Toronto General Hospital for treatment. Again, I do not think that I could have made a big difference in the outcome of the campaign. Although the PCs won the popular vote, the Liberals won the most seats, and their leader Clyde Wells became premier. After much back and forth, Premier Wells broke his word to Prime Minister Mulroney and refused to allow the House of Assembly to vote on the accord. That was the final fatal blow to Meech Lake. Quebec still remains outside the 1982 Constitution.

The enormity of the actions taken by Wells and Harper became evident some five years later in October 1995 as Canadians voted in a referendum on the future of Quebec. I watched that night from Kyrgyzstan as my country came very close to splitting up, mainly because of the rejection of the Meech Lake Accord.

As I reflect back today on the differences that I have been able to make at various levels of politics over the last forty-five years … it becomes clear to me that they dramatically overshadow the number of computers that I would have sold at IBM!

I consider myself to be a very lucky and privileged person to have had the opportunity to help make these differences.

Part of that privilege comes from the opportunities I had to be involved with many outstanding individuals. Each of these has contributed in his or her way, and I will certainly omit someone who should be on this list if I only single out a few by name.

Regardless, the individuals whom I have been most privileged to work with include: Robert Lorne Stanfield (the best prime minister we never had), William Grenville Davis (a class act and effective premier who was loyal to every national and Ontario provincial Conservative leader), John Carnell Crosbie (for his wit and his work for free trade), Brian Mulroney (for his vision, his ability to make a deal, and the fight he led against apartheid in South Africa), Joe Clark (for his support of Newfoundland in the offshore resources issue), Mike Harris (he did what he said he would do), David Miller (a quality individual with vision and integrity, who is dedicated to progressive causes and livable cities), David Smith (who showed me as a young lawyer in Moncton in 1974 what loyalty and courage were all about when he was the first to stand up for his national leader against those in the party who opposed official bilingualism), and Nancy McLean (who taught me the importance of having candidates feel comfortable in their own skins).

This last lesson is what all campaign managers need to remember when they are tempted to convince their candidates to do things that are out of their personal comfort zone.

I said earlier that I would pass on some lessons based upon my experiences. I hope you will agree that I have done that in the preceding chapters of this book. Now, the best way that I can think of to bring this journey to a close is to provide three pieces of advice for those who wish to become successful campaign managers. Yes, it is always a trilogy.

- Associate yourself with quality candidates who have the desire to win regardless of their current standing in the polls. You will be spending a lot of time with them during a very emotional and stressful period, and you will want quality in the room with you during those times.
- Use research wisely and widely to guide the campaign. It is very difficult to plan a political journey without research, and you will never know whether

the journey is off the rails without constantly monitoring its progress. While there are lots of examples in politics where lack of research created significant problems, my favourite story comes from the business world and pollster Martin Goldfarb. An acquaintance told Martin about his plans to build a world-class resort and spa just north of Toronto in the 1980s. Martin asked his friend whether he had conducted any research to determine the market potential for the location and the acceptability of the room rates he would need to charge. His friend said no, and asked Martin how much that type of research would cost. Martin thought about it and said it would be in the ballpark of $30,000. His friend replied, "Thirty thousand dollars! You've got to be kidding! You are just going to make a few phone calls. I don't need that!" When the resort opened it was quickly discovered that there was no market in that location at the price it was charging. The property went into receivership shortly thereafter. I heard later that the total loss was $30 million. His friend's bank today owns the resort and operates it as a training centre for its employees. The $30,000 for research would have served as an insurance premium that could have prevented that huge loss. Financial losses of this magnitude do not occur in politics, but personal careers are regularly broken in the absence of research.

- Listen constantly and do not try to be the smartest person in the room. One simple tactic is to place your work station in the campaign office in the open, not behind a closed door. Not only will it make you more accessible, but you will be perceived by others to always be willing to listen. I credit an experience in 1990 with having taught me about open spaces and accessibility. After Mike Harris won the Ontario PC leadership in 1990, he asked me to run the upcoming provincial election campaign and to be the executive director of the party. During the leadership campaign I had heard a lot of discontent from grassroots party members who felt that headquarters and the staff were inaccessible and disconnected from the party membership. I could see why when I went into headquarters on my first day as executive director. Each person had an office, and each office had a door (usually closed). At the end of my first day I asked to see the building manager of the high-rise building on University Avenue in Toronto where we were renting space. I could not do much about changing the layout of the office without spending a lot of money (which we did not have), but I asked him to take off all the doors that night, including the one to my office, and put them in the basement. Once the staff arrived at 9:00 a.m. the next day, the "open door" story spread quickly to the grassroots of our party. An accessible and open working environment was achieved at party headquarters relatively quickly.

Finally, campaign managers need to remember our place in the political process. Former MP Sam Wakim, a friend and university roommate of Brian Mulroney, likes to say, "It is not the songwriter, it is the singer." The candidate's name is on the ballot. Victory belongs to the candidate, while defeat belongs to us, the campaign managers. Candidates need to live to fight another day. We are dispensable.

When it is all boiled down, politics in a democracy is a contest with active players and referees. The players are the candidates and their campaign supporters. The referees are the voting public who decide on election day who wins the game.

From my experience, the voters are always right — even when I may think they are wrong. Anyone who decides to be a candidate needs to understand that fact of democratic life and to understand the thinking of the voters (referees), because it is they who will ultimately decide the outcome of every election — and because they are always right.

Appendix

John Laschinger's Fifty Campaigns

CANADA

Jean Pigott — 1976 Ottawa-Carleton federal by-election

John C. Crosbie — 1983 PC Party leadership

Brian Mulroney — 1983–84 director of operations in the lead-up to the
    1984 federal election

David MacDonald — 1988 PC Party nomination Toronto Centre-
    Rosedale; 1988 Toronto Centre-Rosedale federal election

Jim Edwards — 1993 PC Party leadership

Joe Clark and PC Party of Canada — 2000 Canada federal election

Peter MacKay — 2003 PC Party leadership

Gary Schellenberger — 2003 Perth-Middlesex federal by-election

Belinda Stronach — 2004 Conservative Party leadership

Brian Topp — 2012 NDP leadership

NEWFOUNDLAND AND LABRADOR

Brian Peckford — 1979 PC Party leadership; 1979, 1982, and 1985 pro-
    vincial elections

Tom Rideout —1989 PC Party leadership and 1989 provincial election

Lynn Verge — 1995 PC Party leadership and 1996 provincial election

NEW BRUNSWICK

Barbara Baird Filliter — 1989 PC Party leadership
Bernard Lord — 1999, 2003, and 2006 provincial elections

NOVA SCOTIA

Tom McInnis — 1991 PC Party leadership

ONTARIO

Larry Grossman — 1985 two PC Party leadership campaigns
Michael Hurst — 1994, 1997, and 2000 Windsor mayoral elections
Mike Harris — 1990 PC Party leadership and 1990 provincial election
June Rowlands — 1991 Toronto mayoral election
Ernie Eves — 2002 PC Party leadership
David Miller — 2003 and 2006 Toronto mayoral elections
John Tory — 2004 PC Party leadership and 2007 provincial election.
Joe Pantalone — 2010 Toronto mayoral election
Olivia Chow — 2014 Toronto mayoral election

MANITOBA

David Brown — 1992 Winnipeg mayoral election
Gary Filmon — 1986 provincial election

ALBERTA

Don Getty — 1985 PC Party leadership
Elaine McCoy— 1992 PC Party leadership
Bill Smith —1992 Edmonton mayoral election

BRITISH COLUMBIA

Bud Smith — 1986 Social Credit Party leadership
Norm Jacobsen — 1991 Social Credit Party leadership

UNITED KINGDOM

John Major — 1997 general election

KYRGYZSTAN

Askar Akayev — 1995 and 2000 presidential elections; 2003 national referendum campaign; 2005 national parliamentary elections, Alga Kyrgyzstan Party

John Laschinger winning record	.600
2015 Toronto Blue Jays winning record	.574

Image Credits

Index

Index

Index

Index

Index

DUNDURN

VISIT US AT

Dundurn.com
@dundurnpress
Facebook.com/dundurnpress
Pinterest.com/dundurnpress